BRARY

5814

8/2010

WITHDRAWN FROM COLLECTION
OF SACRAMENTO PUBLIC LIBRARY

A Chance in Hell

A Chance
in Hell

THE MEN WHO TRIUMPHED
OVER IRAQ'S DEADLIEST CITY
AND TURNED THE TIDE OF WAR

JIM MICHAELS

ST. MARTIN'S PRESS

New York

A CHANCE IN HELL. Copyright © 2010 by Jim Michaels.
All rights reserved. Printed in the United States of America.
For information, address St. Martin's Press,
175 Fifth Avenue, New York, N.Y. 10010.

www.stmartins.com

Map by Paul J. Pugliese

Library of Congress Cataloging-in-Publication Data

Michaels, Jim.
   A chance in Hell : the men who triumphed over Iraq's deadliest city
and turned the tide of war / Jim Michaels.—1st ed.
      p. cm.
   ISBN 978-0-312-58746-8
   1. Iraq War, 2003—Campaigns—Iraq—Ramadi.   2. United States.
Army. Armored Division, 1st.   I. Title.
   DS79.766.R36M527 2010
   956.7044'342—dc22

                                                      2010002173

First Edition: June 2010

10   9   8   7   6   5   4   3   2   1

To the sons of Anbar, Iraqi and American

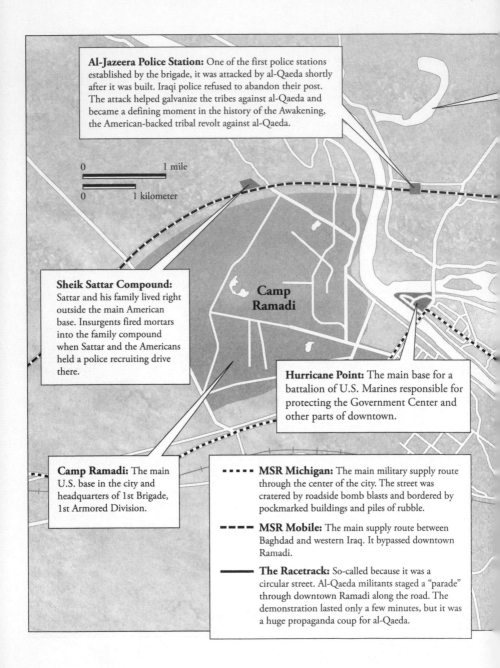

Al-Jazeera Police Station: One of the first police stations established by the brigade, it was attacked by al-Qaeda shortly after it was built. Iraqi police refused to abandon their post. The attack helped galvanize the tribes against al-Qaeda and became a defining moment in the history of the Awakening, the American-backed tribal revolt against al-Qaeda.

0   1 mile

0   1 kilometer

Sheik Sattar Compound: Sattar and his family lived right outside the main American base. Insurgents fired mortars into the family compound when Sattar and the Americans held a police recruiting drive there.

Camp Ramadi

Hurricane Point: The main base for a battalion of U.S. Marines responsible for protecting the Government Center and other parts of downtown.

Camp Ramadi: The main U.S. base in the city and headquarters of 1st Brigade, 1st Armored Division.

MSR Michigan: The main military supply route through the center of the city. The street was cratered by roadside bomb blasts and bordered by pockmarked buildings and piles of rubble.

MSR Mobile: The main supply route between Baghdad and western Iraq. It bypassed downtown Ramadi.

The Racetrack: So-called because it was a circular street. Al-Qaeda militants staged a "parade" through downtown Ramadi along the road. The demonstration lasted only a few minutes, but it was a huge propaganda coup for al-Qaeda.

Ramadi

C-Lake: At one time, this area had a higher concentration of al-Qaeda militants than any other part of Iraq. Insurgents there launched missiles and rockets into Camp Ramadi.

Government Center: By the spring of 2006 Anbar's provincial council and most Ramadi city officials had abandoned the building. Al-Qaeda's wave of assassinations left most government officials dead or intimidated. Only the governor worked there, protected by a company of marines.

Shark Fin: Al-Qaeda militants attacked into the neighborhood in November 2006, torching homes and killing people after the Albu Soda tribe, which lives in the neighborhood, had turned on the insurgents.

Corregidor: The main U.S. base on the east side of Ramadi. When the Albu Soda came under attack, elements of the First Battalion, Ninth Infantry, rushed from the base and drove up the peninsula to the so-called Shark Fin to protect the tribe.

COP Falcon: One of the first combat outposts established inside the city. It came under relentless attack by insurgents, who tried to push the Americans back to their bases outside the city.

CONTENTS

Introduction 1

1. Hero Flight 7

2. Sideshow 21

3. Valley of the Gun 32

4. Back to the Brawl 38

5. Fix Ramadi 50

6. Falcon 64

7. Counterattack 77

8. Sheik Sattar 86

9. Awakening 95

10. "This Is Iraq" 104

11. Secret Talks 121

12. Angel on the Shoulder 134

13. Sympathy for the Devil 145

14. The Chairman's Briefing 162

CONTENTS

15. Shark Fin   *166*

16. Wisam   *177*

17. Justice   *190*

18. Worthy Allies   *200*

19. The Test   *211*

20. Pure Blood   *220*

Notes   *235*

Selected Bibliography   *253*

Where They Are Now   *255*

Acknowledgments   *257*

In Memoriam   *260*

A Chance in Hell

INTRODUCTION

The idea for this book originated during a meeting with a State Department source in the lobby of the Al-Rashid Hotel in Baghdad in the summer of 2006. Sipping thick Turkish coffee amid the the hotel's faded carpets and Saddam-era faux chandeliers, my source talked about strange developments in Ramadi, a provincial capital about seventy miles west of Baghdad. An army brigade commander there was making peace with tribes in the heart of insurgent territory.

The source, who made frequent trips to Anbar and had been in the country for years, wasn't entirely approving of developments there. The brigade commander, Col. Sean MacFarland, was dealing with a minor tribe. His higher command, the Marine Expeditionary Force, was attempting to work with the major sheiks, most of whom had decamped to Amman, Jordan. MacFarland's strategy was showing promise in Ramadi, but threatened to upset the larger strategy in the Sunni province. It wasn't clear where all this was heading.

The story was intriguing, though I was skeptical it had the broad implications necessary for a cover story in *USA Today*. At best it was a bright spot amid a war that was going poorly. It was hard to be optimistic about Iraq in 2006. At best, Ramadi would make an interesting color story; shades of T. E. Lawrence. There was something romantic about desert tribes. I asked a few questions, flipped my notebook shut, and walked from the lobby's chilled air into the Baghdad summer. I was finishing up a reporting trip and it would be several months before I was back in Iraq. I figured the story could wait.

I was wrong. Within months, Ramadi had gone from an insurgent safe haven to a model of stability. The turnaround was largely ignored by the media at the time and was overshadowed by unrelenting bad news elsewhere in Iraq and policy gridlock in Washington.

What happened? I got a chance to find out in the spring of 2007 when I heard that an army team was going to Germany to gather lessons learned from MacFarland's First Brigade, First Armored Division, which had just returned from Ramadi to its base in Friedberg, Germany. Col. Steve Mains, director of the Center for Army Lessons Learned, without hesitation allowed me to accompany the team to Germany. I spent several days interviewing commanders, staff officers, and noncommissioned officers in the bucolic setting of the German countryside.

It was hard to escape the conclusion that the success in Ramadi was more about the art—not the science—of war. It was a story about leadership and how the decisions of individuals can change the tide of history.

The idea of a peaceful Ramadi seemed far-fetched when the brigade first arrived. The city looked like Stalingrad under seige. There was no other way to describe it. Americans were lobbing rockets into the center of the city on a regular basis. Anbar

Province was a sideshow. The real effort was in Baghdad. Other units and commanders came and went in Ramadi. MacFarland saw something many others missed. He didn't fall back on regulations and policy guidance. He was given latitude and he took every inch of it. When his higher command wanted to put the brakes on his initiative, he pushed back.

MacFarland was only part of the equation. The other half of this remarkable story was Abdul Sattar Bezia al-Rishawi. Sheik Sattar was easy to overlook. He was a minor sheik and the head of a small tribe. He carried around a six-shooter and liked whiskey. A cautious military commander would keep the likes of Sattar at a distance.

MacFarland embraced the sheik. Sattar returned the embrace. It's hard to overestimate how crucial—and courageous—that decision was for both men. When the war looked hopeless these two men helped changed the course of history. That is not to take away from anything that has happened before or since. But this story reminds us all that wars are won and lost by men and women and the decisions they make.

It is wrong to think of this as an American initiative. It was a tribal revolt against al-Qaeda. But MacFarland made the very risky decision to support it. History would have been different had he made another call.

What happened in Ramadi in 2006 is not well understood.

Even as it became clear that Ramadi was improving dramatically in late 2006, Baghdad and other parts of Iraq continued to slide downhill. The policy for Iraq in Washington was in disarray. In January 2007 the White House announced a new strategy backed by temporary reinforcements of 30,000 "surge" forces that would be deployed to Iraq. Most of the troops were headed toward the capital. The developments in Ramadi would soon be overshadowed by a massive flow of American troops into Iraq under the new plan.

The story of the surge and MacFarland's experience in Ramadi would briefly surface as an issue in the 2008 presidential campaign. Senator John McCain had tied his political fortunes to the White House's surge strategy. McCain's critics said the developments in Ramadi in 2006 proved that progress in Iraq had started *before* the surge, suggesting the new method was irrelevant at best.

This book will likely reignite the debate. That would be too bad. The argument missed the point, as political squabbles often do. MacFarland's Ready First Brigade succeeded because they were using the tactics of the surge—though officially the strategy had not been launched yet. Gen. David Petraeus, who was appointed to lead the new U.S. effort in Iraq, institutionalized those tactics across Iraq, averting disaster and putting the war on a path toward victory.

There had been other successful efforts at reconciliation, dating back to 2003 when Petraeus was a division commander and was reaching out to former Baathists. In 2005, Marine Lt. Col. Dale Alford formed an alliance with the tribes and pushed al-Qaeda out of al-Qaim, a small city near the border of Syria. An army brigade in Tal Afar, in northern Iraq, built a model of stability by forming alliances with local leaders. But MacFarland's alliance with Sheik Sattar defeated al-Qaeda in a strategically important city. This model of cooperation to end al-Qaeda's presence in Iraq was supported by Petraeus and soon there were awakenings across the country.

Iraqis felt no sympathy for al-Qaeda, but they weren't confident the Americans were reliable allies. MacFarland and Sattar—two unlikely partners—changed the battlefield calculus in Iraq.

The confusion over the significance of the awakening in Ramadi is unfortunate. There are lessons to be drawn from what happened there. Some are applicable in Afghanistan—a place that looks as hopeless as Iraq did in 2006.

Winning hearts and minds is a misleading slogan. This is not about convincing people that democracy or capitalism is superior to other systems. It is about an alignment of interests. Tribes in Iraq changed sides only when they were convinced that America was a reliable partner, that the United States would not leave and that it would ultimately prevail.

Most solutions are local. No one wanted to live under al-Qaeda, but until we gave people a means of defending themselves they had no choice other than to throw in their lot with the insurgents. Once they had an alternative, events moved quickly. But the security originated with the tribes, villages, and neighborhoods. There was no grand compromise at the national level.

Firepower shouldn't be used indiscriminately, but it is an important part of winning an insurgency. The hard-core militants have to be killed or captured and the population has to be convinced that America is capable of doing the job. The soldiers of the Ready First weren't afraid to use overwhelming firepower—including manuevering tanks through city streets—when it was necessary. That helped convince those sitting on the fence that al-Qaeda might not win in the war.

It is too early to declare victory in Iraq. There are plenty of things that could go wrong. The Americans helped empower these tribes and if the Shiite-led government reneges on promises made to the Sunnis in Anbar it could lead to a violent backlash, one that Americans will be powerless to defuse. There are other dangers. The Sunnis might fight among themselves if newly empowered tribes use their influence to marginalize rivals. If that happens historians may look back on Anbar as a positive footnote in an otherwise grim story. It's easy to predict disaster in Iraq. The country will be working through problems, sometimes violently, for years to come.

But there is a forward momentum that will be difficult, perhaps impossible, to reverse. Iraqis are tired of fighting and are beginning to taste a better life. My prediction is that we will look back on Anbar as the place where the United States got it right.

1

Hero Flight

Behold, as may unworthiness define,
A little touch of Harry in the night.
—HENRY V

The doors opened, spilling a pool of yellow light into the darkness. Four stretcher bearers came out with the remains of Private First Class Brett Tribble, zipped into a black plastic body bag. The soldiers stood in two ranks, lining the gravel road in front of the makeshift morgue—a plywood building equipped with extra air conditioners to keep the bodies cool. First Sgt. David Shaw called the men to attention and the soldiers saluted as the stretcher bearers moved slowly down the ranks. It was silent, except for the scrape of the litter-bearers' boots against the gravel road.

Capt. Artie Maxwell, the battalion chaplain, recited the Twenty-third Psalm: "Yea, though I walk through the valley of the shadow of death . . ." The stretcher bearers—four noncommissioned officers from Tribble's company—placed his body carefully in the back of a waiting field ambulance. The two ranks then closed into one and formed a procession behind the ambulance, which turned left and drove slowly toward the helicopter landing zone, about a hundred yards away. Small green chemlites placed on the side of the road marked the path dimly.

The drone of the helicopters grew deafening as the birds approached the landing zone. A pair of Marine Corps CH-46s closed in, their gray drab airframes barely lighter than the dark sky. In 2006, most helicopters in Anbar Province flew at night with their running lights off to avoid ground fire. They didn't remain on the ground long. The camp was often the target of enemy rocket and mortar fire. The helicopters hovered briefly and then settled on the sand, squatting in the darkness as their blades continued to turn, violently stirring the warm air and sending out a blast of small rocks and debris. Guided by the helicopter's helmeted crew chief, the stretcher bearers crouched and moved through the rotor wash toward the back of the bird, carefully placing Tribble's remains on board and then walking off the landing zone. The soldiers came to attention and saluted a last time. The ramp closed, the engines whined, and the helicopters hesitated briefly before climbing, kicking up another blast of debris in their wake and forcing the soldiers to turn their heads away.

The aircraft climbed until they were swallowed by the darkness.

Tribble was raised in a small town south of Houston and his parents made a living off the chemical plants that cluster along the Gulf Coast. His mother worked in an office as an expediter and his father as a pipe fabricator. They divorced when he was thirteen, and Tribble and his two brothers were raised by his mom.

At age fourteen he was in a car with two buddies. One of them poked his upper body through the car's sunroof and fired a .38 pistol at the home of a girl who had jilted him. For Tribble it was the beginning of a troubled period during which he was in and out of juvenile detention facilities. He had spent so much time in juvenile detention he couldn't fit back into high school. He tried his hand at pipe fitting work with his dad and enrolled for a time in welder's school. Neither worked.

At seventeen, he found himself without a job or a high school diploma—and with a pregnant girlfriend who wasn't sure she wanted to stay with him.

His mother, Tracy Tribble, came home from work and found him lying on his bed, crying.

"Mom, I don't know what I'm going to do."

It was odd. He wasn't one to express his feelings. His mother figured he had got a glimpse of his future and had panicked. Pending fatherhood had focused his mind.

His mother suggested the army. She had read about the military and how it provided direction and discipline to young men without either. "Let them show you the world," she said. "Let them pay for your education."

He said nothing.

Several months later, Tribble told his mother he had enlisted in the U.S. Army. The recruiter had worked to have some of the felonies on his record dropped to misdemeanors and he was off to basic training.

He returned a changed person. He had lost the chip on his shoulder and seemed more at ease, less angry. His mother hoped the changes were for good. Tribble signed up for the infantry even though his recruiter told him there were lots of other options in the army. He was good at infantry skills and the army meant steady pay.

His mom, stepmother, and brother Clint drove to Fort Benning, Georgia, to see him graduate from infantry training. Tracy Tribble choked back tears as she watched the band, the cannon fire, and the rest of the pageantry.

Tribble received orders to a battalion in Germany that was getting ready for another Iraq tour. It was his first time on a plane and he landed wide-eyed in Europe. The base was huge, with all the comforts of an American town. He and his friends explored the country. He told his mom about taking a train ride and eating in a restaurant that was hundreds of years old.

"You ought to see this place," he told her over the phone.

"I need to get promoted so I can be making some money for my boy," Tribble told his friend, Jason Dickerson, a medic.

He had an easy personality that drew people to him and he was good at what he did. He had found a home.

His battalion was sent to Kuwait, where it served as part of the "strategic reserve." It wouldn't go to Iraq unless things were going bad.

The Pentagon had expected a short war to overthrow Saddam's regime. By 2006 America was faced with a growing insurgency and sectarian violence that threatened to engulf Iraq in a civil war. The military, which had shrunk dramatically after the cold war, was struggling to come up with enough troops to deal with the twin challenges in Iraq.

In 2006, Gen. George Cascy, the top U.S. commander in Iraq, decided to commit his reserves to the fight. He had no choice. Things were spiraling out of control. Tribble's battalion, 1-35 Armor, would go to Ramadi, the provincial capital of Anbar Province and the heart of the Sunni insurgency. Tribble and his friends had followed the news while in Kuwait. They had seen the television images from Ramadi. They knew it was Iraq's deadliest city.

Tribble's mom took his call at work. She rushed into the company cafeteria where she could talk privately. Her son told her they were in a really bad area. He couldn't say more.

Tribble had been in Iraq less than a week when he volunteered to man the gunner's hatch on a night patrol planned for Ramadi's Tameem neighborhood, one of the city's worst areas. He was supposed to be a "dismount," meaning he would sit in the back of the vehicle and only get out when required for a foot patrol. Tribble asked if he could be a gunner instead. Dismounts were little more than passengers until action happened. Standing in the gunner's hatch with your body partially exposed was more dangerous. That's where Tribble wanted to be.

Sgt. Tom Davis, the squad leader, and Dickerson were leaning over a map spread on the hood of a Humvee, going over that evening's patrol. Tribble came over and draped his arm over Dickerson and peered at the map. Dickerson could tell he was excited.

"I'm gunning tonight," Tribble said with a grin.

Dickerson, twenty-two, was less gung ho. He had had a previous combat tour in Baghdad. As a medic, his job forced him to dwell on war's ugly side. When the unit was in Kuwait, Lt. Col. John Farr, the battalion doctor, called the medics into a meeting in a large tent when they learned they were heading to Ramadi.

"You guys are going to the most dangerous city in the most dangerous country in the world right now," Farr told them. "You're going to see combat."

Dickerson was in no hurry to get back to Iraq.

The patrol rolled out of Camp Ramadi at about 9 P.M., with three Humvees and two Bradleys, large heavily armored vehicles. The Bradleys went off and established fixed checkpoints in the darkened streets and the Humvees rolled farther into Tameem. A Humvee with National Guard soldiers from the unit they were replacing accompanied the patrol for part of the way, but they also moved off to set up a checkpoint. It was their last night patrolling the city before heading home. They didn't want to take unnecessary risks and they were in a hurry to get out of Ramadi. Tribble's battalion had just arrived in Iraq from Kuwait and hadn't even officially taken over the "battle space" yet.

The military calls this kind of handoff a "relief in place," and it is considered one of the most dangerous operations a unit can perform. It thickens the fog of war as a new group attempts to step into the role of the departing unit while the enemy continues attacking.

That left the new men to feel their way along unfamiliar streets. Davis and his men frequently checked maps inside their darkened vehicles, trying to identify what roads were passable and what routes they had been warned to avoid.

It had been a long day for the new men, who had been working in the hot sun since 7 A.M. The soldiers had been scrambling since they had arrived from Kuwait. The company had received some Humvees from another unit and had to inspect each one. They had to bolt additional armor onto the Bradleys. Then during last-minute checks, they discovered that there were problems with the radios. Davis had communication with the other Humvees in his patrol, but only sporadically with his platoon leader. Patrols had to be on the streets 24/7. There was no way they could pause for several days to get their bearings.

Davis had had a previous tour in Baghdad and noticed the difference as soon as he landed in Ramadi. In Baghdad, children would wave at patrols. Even adults would occasionally smile at American soldiers.

"I had seen what it was like when people actually liked us," Davis said.

Ramadi was different. The streets were piled with trash and cratered in places by roadside bombs. Buildings were pockmarked or crumbling. This looked like a combat zone; like a city under siege.

"As soon as you turned the corner and walked down a street, people scattered like something bad was going to happen or they just didn't want to be around you."

Even women on the streets shot hostile looks or glared as the Americans patrolled the streets. There were no friendlies.

"No one even wanted to spit in your direction," Davis said.

The darkened Humvees were driving by an apartment complex when one of the soldiers reported seeing a man hunkered down and observing the patrol. He could have been a roadside bomb triggerman or an observer who would alert insurgents to an approaching American patrol. There was a strict nighttime curfew and under the rules of engagement a man out at night tracking an American patrol could be considered hostile. The patrol fired a burst from a machine gun, but the man slipped back into the shadows.

The patrol rolled on, the men feeling their way through Ramadi's strange streets.

Davis felt uneasy in the lead vehicle. It was his first night patrol since arriving in Ramadi. He pulled over and let a sergeant who knew the roads better take the lead. That sergeant took a wrong turn, backed up, and the patrol resumed behind him. Dickerson was driving the last vehicle, following Davis. The unfamiliar streets looked eerie through the night vision scope, which casts everything in a dim green tint.

"Man, I do not like these streets," said Cpl. Alonzo Epps, who was riding in the Humvee with Dickerson.

Dickerson kept his eyes on the road. There is a balance between staying hyperaware of your surroundings and freaking out.

"If you think about shit too long it starts getting to you," is the way Dickerson puts it.

But Dickerson was also having a hard time keeping the uneasy feelings at bay.

"I don't know where the hell we are right now," he told Epps.

The patrol turned right. There were piles of trash on the

road. To the left were homes and to the right a brick wall surrounding a schoolyard. The street ended in a T-intersection. The first vehicle turned left. Davis's vehicle approached the intersection and was about to turn.

It was not a sharp, loud explosion, but a deep percussion that shook the earth. That's how Dickerson knew it was bad. The smaller roadside bombs are louder. This one was buried deep in the ground and the blast was directed upward into the Humvee's vulnerable underside. Davis's Humvee with Tribble in the turret took the blast full on, sending the vehicle two stories high before it flipped over backward and crashed on to the street in front of Dickerson. The harsh thud of the five-ton vehicle hitting the concrete road was louder than the explosion. A mushroom cloud of dust and debris rose from the road where the roadside bomb had been.

Dickerson was right behind the Humvee. He didn't bother hitting the brakes. He threw the vehicle into park, grabbed his equipment bag, pushed open the heavy door, and sprinted toward the Humvee, which lay upside down in front of him. Dickerson had been trained to check for "secondary" bombs that are sometimes placed by insurgents to kill or maim people who rush to the scene of an attack. Using a flashlight, he slowed down and scanned the side of the road as he approached the Humvee.

When he reached the vehicle he saw that the Humvee lay across Tribble's lower body. His eyes were closed, but he was taking short raspy breaths. His face was blue. Tribble was taking his last breaths.

The passenger side door was blown off or broke off when it hit the ground. Davis was lying upside down in the vehicle, moaning. His face was bloody and his nose was swollen. Dickerson ran his flashlight over him to assess his injuries. There was a lot of blood around his left leg, but he would have to get the sergeant out of the Humvee to look at it.

Dickerson then poked his head into the vehicle and yelled, "Somebody talk to me!"

Pvt. 1st Class Adam Hailey was in the driver's seat, but couldn't get out.

"Doc!" Hailey screamed. "Get me the fuck out of here!"

Dickerson also needed to get Davis out quick. The lights and noise were sure to attract insurgents eager to take potshots at the Americans gathered at the intersection. But Davis was wrapped in the seat belt and squeezed amid the wreckage of the Humvee. The job was made even more difficult because Dickerson had to reach across a large crater where the bomb had detonated. Finally, Dickerson jumped into the hole and grabbed Davis under the arms.

"Sergeant Davis, you're going to have to take your right leg and give the biggest kick you can," Dickerson told him.

Davis pushed with his right leg, pulling free from the Humvee and landing on top of Dickerson in the bomb crater. The crater was filling with water from a broken pipe.

Dickerson dragged Davis out of the hole and looked at his leg. His knee was mostly gone. His leg was still attached, but Dickerson saw little hope that it could be saved. He had a broken hand and nose and a dislocated arm. Dickerson was worried that Davis had other injuries that he couldn't see with his flashlight.

Davis was conscious and began asking Dickerson a series of

questions. He wanted to know if the men in his squad were okay. As Dickerson frantically examined Davis's wounds and applied a tourniquet above his left knee, Davis demanded to know if the equipment in the Humvee was secured. Soldiers are trained to secure or destroy any sensitive equipment to ensure it doesn't fall into the enemy's hands.

Dickerson tightened the tourniquet with every ounce of strength he had so Davis wouldn't lose any more blood. Davis shuddered from the pain. The medic had no morphine to provide Davis. He had asked the company medic for a supply earlier in the day and was told they would work on the request. Now he wished he had been more insistent.

"We were getting too much responsibility too fast," Dickerson says.

He was making mental notes of what he would need now that his platoon was in the Ramadi fight.

Dickerson told Davis the men in his squad were all okay, even though Tribble lay dying only yards away. He told him the equipment was secured. Davis seemed relieved. "Strange," Dickerson thought. Davis was losing blood, in pain, and about to lose his leg, and yet all he could think of was the welfare of his men and accounting for their equipment.

"Am I going to lose my leg?" Davis asked finally.

"No," Dickerson said. "You'll be fine." He knew that too was probably a lie.

It was about then that insurgents from the nearby apartments opened fire on the Americans. Soldiers manning machine guns on the surviving two Humvees quickly fired back, killing two militants. The firing stopped.

Dickerson got Davis into the back of a Bradley and they raced to the field hospital on Camp Ramadi. The soldiers were so new to the area they had to follow the signs on the base to the hospital.

Dickerson hadn't reported Tribble's death on the radio, and even at the scene, when Sgt. David Enstad had walked around the Humvee toward Tribble, he had intercepted him and steered him away. He was worried that if people around him found out they would freak out.

Now he met up with the platoon leader, Sgt. 1st Class Mike Harris, and broke the news. He told him the other men were fine, but they would need to go back into the city to extract the rest of the squad and Tribble's body.

They were getting ready to go back out when Harris turned to Dickerson. "Are you okay?" Dickerson looked at his uniform. He was soaked in Davis's blood.

"Yeah, I'm fine I guess."

When Dickerson returned to the intersection, he asked the medics on the scene if they had a body bag. It was something else he had forgotten. They didn't have one. He ran over to the Humvee with the National Guard unit, who were just wrapping up a twelve-month tour in Ramadi. They brought one.

A recovery vehicle had arrived and lifted the Humvee off Tribble. A few soldiers helped Dickerson place Tribble's body into the bag. The medic knelt down and looked a last time at his friend's lifeless face. Tribble was two months short of his twenty-first birthday.

"Sorry, man," Dickerson said.

He zipped the bag closed.

———

The hero flight—Maj. Michael Wood, the brigade chaplain, had changed the name from angel flight because theology didn't support the idea of men becoming angels—is the first step to returning fallen soldiers to their homes. Memorial services and other remembrances would come later. Tonight about a hundred men—most of Company B, except the troops who were out on patrol that night—came to see Tribble off. The clatter of the helicopters soon faded to a buzz barely distinguishable from the camp's background noise—the constant drone of generators and diesel engines. By 10 P.M. the brutal daytime temperatures that exceed a hundred degrees had dropped to the low seventies. It was clear and the stars were brilliant.

Dickerson watched the helicopter leave. Uneasy thoughts flooded his mind. He knew there had been no way to save Tribble, but would the other members of his platoon know that? *Would they trust him?*

Col. Sean MacFarland, forty-seven, the brigade commander in Ramadi, emerged from the darkness. Lanky, with a shock of brown hair, MacFarland had none of the physical swagger of a George Patton. In civilian clothes he could pass for a high-school science teacher.

MacFarland had also just arrived in Ramadi days earlier. Tribble's battalion was part of the task force under MacFarland's First Brigade, First Armored Division.

MacFarland heard quiet sobs and sniffles from the men

who had just loaded Tribble's body onto the marine helicopter. Others were angry, swearing and vowing revenge. Many were new to combat. They were not sure how to respond to their first loss.

MacFarland startled the troops. He walked down the row of soldiers, asking how each one was doing. Most had not seen their brigade commander and didn't know who he was until he got close enough that they could see the eagle on his uniform. The act of telling the colonel they were okay and hearing their buddies saying the same thing seemed to help. MacFarland knew that young soldiers are resilient and can recover from a combat death, but it usually takes a few days.

He also knew they didn't have that kind of time. Many of Tribble's buddies would be going back out on patrol in a matter of hours.

There was no time to grieve.

2

Sideshow

If men make war in slavish obedience to rules, they
will fail.

—ULYSSES S. GRANT

At 7 A.M., May 22, 2006, MacFarland touched down in
Camp Ramadi in a blast of heat and sand. Temperatures
were already exceeding a hundred degrees when he climbed out
of the Black Hawk helicopter. He dumped his pack, grabbed
something to eat, and joined his new boss, Marine Maj. Gen.
Richard Zilmer, on a drive to meet the governor and get a first
glimpse of the city.

The convoy left the compound and turned on to the main
thoroughfare, called Route Michigan by the U.S. military. Mac-
Farland peered out of the thick blast-proof window of his armored Humvee. The shells of burnt-out vehicles lined the road,
along with chunks of concrete and piles of garbage. The streets

were mostly empty of people. Every single building they passed
was scarred by war.

They found the governor at his compound in the center of
town. He was living in a fortress, surrounded by concrete blast
walls, razor wire, and machine-gun emplacements. The area was
protected by U.S. Marines. MacFarland and his security team
sprinted from their vehicles into the compound because of the
constant threat from snipers nesting in abandoned buildings
across the street. Even inside the small compound, marines had
to dash across the small courtyard when they moved between
buildings to avoid snipers firing into the tiny perimeter at the
heart of Ramadi. Gov. Mamoun Sami Rashid al-Alwani sat
behind a largely empty desk in a cavernous office in a building
with only sporadic power. He had no visitors. MacFarland could
see why. Nobody in their right mind would do business at the
government center. Even if they made it in, insurgents watching from outside the complex would surely kill them when
they left.

Al-Qaeda had successfully chipped away at the provincial
government through regular assassinations. Anbar's provincial
council met in Baghdad's fortified Green Zone, seventy miles
away. Ramadi was too dangerous. A number of council members had already been killed. Most city officials had also long
since abandoned the city, except for a few who slept in the government center during the week and then fled to homes in
Baghdad and elsewhere for the weekends. Downtown Ramadi
was abandoned by everyone except the insurgents who lurked in
the crumbling wreckage of the city.

Keeping the governor alive required an entire company of

marines, more than a hundred men, who were assigned to protect the government center and take Mamoun between home and work. Marines arrayed with a slew of infantry weapons were positioned on the roof, each man responsible for a sector. Someone had even scrounged an aging M79 grenade launcher, called a blooper by infantrymen in Vietnam, because it was well suited for the urban jungle of Ramadi.

Any time the governor left the compound, marines ferried him in an armored convoy. It was dangerous work. The marine company assigned to protect the government center had lost five men in three months by the time MacFarland arrived. They had kept the governor alive. He had survived more than thirty assassination attempts. But he was a prisoner of his own security. If the Americans lost Mamoun there would be no government left.

"He's a government of one," MacFarland concluded.

After visiting the governor, MacFarland went to check on an ongoing police recruitment drive. It wasn't going much better. The U.S.-sponsored drive was supposed to recruit 240 officers. They had forty applicants in two days. Joining the police in Ramadi was suicide.

American strategy at the time was to turn security and government responsibilities over to the Iraqis as soon as possible. In Ramadi, the provincial capital of Iraq's most important Sunni province, there was no government or police force. There was nobody to turn responsibility over to. It was a strategy in name only.

On Sunday, June 26, about a month after MacFarland arrived, he was told that about $7 million had disappeared from the Rafidain Bank in downtown Ramadi. It was the only functioning bank in the city. No one had a good answer for how it happened, though it was clearly an inside job. The money was to pay government pensions for workers at the glass factory, now abandoned. "That didn't make sense either," MacFarland thought.

"They were getting paid to sit around and make bombs to kill Americans."

MacFarland graduated from West Point in 1981, on the eve of President Ronald Reagan's massive military buildup. By the time Reagan took over, the all-volunteer U.S. military was already healing from the scars of Vietnam. The Vietnam-era draft brought in thousands of young men, many of whom would rather be doing something else. The armed forces were gripped by discipline, drug, and racial problems. Compounding the difficulties was the inequity with which the draft was applied. Affluent students could easily get a deferment in the latter years of the war, leaving the draft to target low-income and minority recruits. The Vietnam War was one of America's most unpopular military campaigns and much of the country's anger was directed at the soldiers and marines almost as much as at Congress and the White House. The armed forces limped out of Vietnam, unsure of themselves and with much of their swagger gone.

The new president chose to come to West Point on a hazy spring day to address the class of 1981, soon after he took office. He promised to sweep away the "Vietnam syndrome," replacing it with a new sense of optimism. "In much of the 1970s, there was a widespread lack of respect for the uniform, born perhaps by what has been called the Vietnam syndrome," Reagan told the 906 graduates, including 58 women, at West Point. This class would enter a new military, a military that was not carrying the burden of America's defeat in Southeast Asia. He pledged to boost pay and restore respect to the military profession, triggering a loud round of applause. Money would go for salaries, training, and equipment.

The military would be at the vanguard of a new spirit of optimism in the country.

"The era of self-doubt is over," the president declared.

MacFarland was the son and grandson of army officers and had grown up in an Irish Catholic enclave of Albany, New York, and later Canajoharie, a small town amid the dairy farms of upstate New York. He was a water sports enthusiast who had planned on going to the U.S. Naval Academy, but changed his mind at the last minute because the navy required a waiver for his eyesight and the army didn't. He entered the armor branch because tanks "are the closest things to ships the army has."

By the 1980s, the U.S. military had settled into the rhythm of a peacetime army of inspections and training. As a newly minted lieutenant, MacFarland chafed under the strict rules and regulations that are everywhere when the nation is not at war. His career got off to a rocky start. By the time he was a junior captain he had collected several letters of reprimand. One of the reprimands was for not providing a sufficient amount of supervision when he was running a pistol range. America's all-volunteer military had developed a zero-defect mentality that often discouraged taking chances and bred a nanny culture within the ranks. MacFarland thought cavalry soldiers could be given more responsibility and didn't need the level of hand-holding that had become routine in the peacetime military. Cavalry soldiers are supposed to be trained to make decisions on the fly, without seeking authorization.

"How does it make sense to say that, on the one hand, and then on the other we can't trust you to clear your own pistol?

"The more time we spent garrisoned, the more centralized we became," MacFarland said.

MacFarland was introverted and cerebral in a branch that prized cigar-chomping, hard-drinking commanders. Armor units trace their lineage to the horse cavalry and they wear Stetsons and spurs. During a tour in Germany MacFarland served under J. W. Thurman, a legendary cavalry officer who had won a Distinguished Service Cross in Vietnam. Thurman named one of his sons after George Patton. MacFarland wound up in his squadron as a staff officer in charge of logistics. One day when Thurman's tanks were going to the range, an ammunition truck had a flat tire and got there late. Thurman was apoplectic. He turned on the skinny young staff officer with a rebellious streak, screaming at him and some of his colleagues in the logistics shop. He followed it with a letter calling MacFarland "a marble-headed motherfucker."

Part of the problem was MacFarland's attitude as a young officer. He was perhaps too dismissive of the army's conventional ways and a bit cocky, too quick to rebel. "As a twenty-three- and twenty-four-year-old lieutenant I was pretty sure I had it all figured out.

"My future was not bright," MacFarland says.

He intended to stay in the army, but he was looking for his place in it. He wasn't a loud, swashbuckling commander. "I am not George Patton and never could be," MacFarland said. "If I tried to come off looking like George Patton I'd have looked like a big phony." He was devouring Civil War history when he picked up Ulysses S. Grant's memoir. Grant was quiet and understated. *He couldn't stand the sight of blood.* Yet he turned the tide for the Union army through sheer force of will. He forged ahead despite repeated setbacks. His quiet demeanor masked a determination of cast iron.

It was an epiphany for the young officer. "I could be a guy like that," MacFarland thought.

MacFarland found his footing in the army and was prized for his intellect and competence. He was quietly ambitious, and rose through the ranks in a succession of key commands. The reprimands were "local" and so were not included in his official record book. Even Thurman changed his mind and rewarded him with a command in his squadron. The dressing-down was just a "wake-up call," Thurman recalls.

America's military in the 1980s, when the cold war was still raging, was trained and organized for conventional war. There would be surrogate wars in Central America, Africa, and elsewhere, but the main thrust would be preparing for a conventional war against the Soviet bloc. At the heart of that mission were America's armored units, which were designed to blunt a Soviet mechanized attack across the plains of Europe. Light infantry and the marines might train occasionally for smaller wars, but the armored units were designed for one job: taking on the Soviets.

America's military—like the nation—did its best to forget

the trauma of Vietnam. What emerged from the ashes of Vietnam was the Powell Doctrine, the concept that the United States would only fight wars where it could use overwhelming force and had the full backing of the American public. Guerrilla wars were synonymous with quagmires.

America would prepare for wars it was confident it could win.

The U.S. military was reduced in size when the cold war ended, but little was decided about its new mission. The 1991 Persian Gulf War only reinforced the viability of the Powell Doctrine. America's advantage in technology and firepower would win wars. America would avoid conflicts unless it could use these advantages.

America's enemies would ultimately draw the same conclusions. Osama bin Laden and his followers saw the United States withdraw from Vietnam, Lebanon, and then Somalia. It was best to draw America into a protracted guerrilla war. Americans don't have the stomach for unconventional combat where the battle lines aren't clearly drawn. The way to beat America, they figured, was to draw it into a back-alley knife fight.

In 2003, shortly after the U.S.-led invasion of Iraq, MacFarland was assigned as an operations officer to the staff of Lt. Gen. Ricardo Sanchez, who was commanding coalition forces. MacFarland watched the war unfold from coalition military headquarters in Baghdad.

"It was like watching a slow-motion train wreck."

Armed resistance to the U.S. presence was growing, but there was mostly denial in Washington.

"It was kind of confusing to hear our political masters on TV saying things like, 'There is no insurgency and they're just dead-enders.'

"That wasn't what we were seeing."

Sanchez was constantly battling the Pentagon, arguing against removing brigades without replacing them. But the command hadn't come up with a plan to confront the new reality.

"We didn't really have a strategy at that point."

Like others on the staff, MacFarland was trying to get a handle on what was happening. "We were trying to figure out what we were up against and what to do about it."

A visiting analyst from a Washington think tank asked MacFarland if things were improving. "At best we're moving sideways," MacFarland told him.

Three years later the war was no longer drifting sideways. Violence was spiraling out of control.

MacFarland came back to Iraq in January 2006 as commander of the First Brigade, First Armored Division, one of the massive armored forces trained and organized to stop the Soviets at the Fulda Gap. MacFarland never lost a fondness for misfits with unconventional ideas—the result of his own rocky early career. His unit was first sent to Tal Afar, in northern Iraq. Shortly after arriving, he approved a plan to place photos of al-Qaeda leaders on posters around town, saying they were wanted on charges of pedophilia, homosexuality, and alcohol abuse—the worst crimes imaginable in the eyes of Muslims.

Operation Bridge Builder, as it was called, worked. A number of al-Qaeda leaders fled the city. MacFarland figured the operation was justified because interrogations revealed that the suspects were drug abusers and pedophiles. It was the kind of outlandish idea that appealed to MacFarland. It may also reflect a piety that came from a strict Catholic upbringing. It wasn't hard for him to link the enemy's brutal tactics with a deeper moral depravity.

By the time MacFarland arrived in Ramadi the Iraq war was looking increasingly hopeless. Violence was growing throughout the country. Ramadi had become a capital for the Sunni insurgency.

Maj. Teddy Gates, a marine officer, was skeptical when he first met MacFarland in Ramadi. He wasn't what Gates expected. Ramadi was a violent place, and he thought the new commander would possess an overpowering presence and bravado. MacFarland spoke quietly and had a dry sense of humor. He rarely raised his voice. He didn't talk about kicking the enemy's ass.

"Who sent this guy here?" Gates thought. "Does he have any idea what we're up against? There's no way he will get it done. Can we have a killer around here?" Gates would later come to consider him the best officer he served under.

At a staff meeting shortly after arriving in Ramadi, Lt. Col. Pete Lee, the brigade's executive officer, asked MacFarland what the brigade's goal should be. MacFarland wasn't aiming for an exit strategy. He thought al-Qaeda could be defeated on their home turf. "Peace and prosperity in Ramadi," MacFarland told Lee.

Anbar was viewed differently from the U.S. command in

Baghdad. Ramadi was an "economy of force" mission—a sideshow, in military-speak. It would be enough to stabilize the city to choke off the weapons and foreign fighters that were flowing from Syria through the western desert to Baghdad, the military's main effort. Most American news reports described Ramadi as "insurgent held." It wasn't far from the truth.

"Al Anbar is going to be one of the last provinces to be stabilized," predicted Lt. Gen. John F. Sattler, who oversaw marine forces in the Middle East and Central Asia, shortly after MacFarland's brigade took over in Ramadi.

"The silver lining is that it lowers expectations for me," MacFarland thought a week after arriving.

The Pentagon asked MacFarland to brief reporters on a videoconference from Iraq shortly after arriving in Ramadi. Halfway into the press conference, a UPI reporter was called on by the moderator in the Pentagon pressroom.

"Can you explain to us why Ramadi continues to be such a problem?" she asked. "And why do you think you're going to be the one that's going to be able to turn this around?"

3

Valley of the Gun

Strength does not come from physical capacity. It comes from an indomitable will.

—MOHANDAS GANDHI

The man stared for a few seconds at his chest, where he had been shot six times.

He lifted his head and looked straight at Sgt. Jesus Cadena, who had done the shooting. It had happened so fast. Cadena returned the stare, noting where the bullets entered the man's torso. There was no blood. The small rounds from Cadena's M4 passed right through his body. The man fell to one knee and collapsed on the floor.

The fight wasn't over. There were at least two other armed men inside the house.

Cadena's patrol had entered Tameem, a neighborhood in eastern Ramadi, before dawn on September 28, 2006. The idea was to be in position when the sun came up in order to maintain an element of surprise as the patrol entered homes and began questioning people.

By midmorning it was getting hot. The men—there were about a dozen in the patrol—walked on either side of the dirt street, keeping a distance between them. There was a slight mist that would burn off as the day wore on. Cinder block homes were crowded together on both sides of the street. The homes were hidden behind concrete walls that were entered through large swinging metal gates. Families were waking up and women had begun baking flatbread in large brick ovens inside the courtyards. The smell drifted down the street. The soldiers had already visited about five homes by 10 A.M. They would typically post a couple of men on the roof and position other soldiers outside for security. The squad leader would take a knee or sit in a plastic chair, talking to whoever headed the family.

The families were not uncooperative, but they were wary. They had seen Americans pass by the neighborhood, but this was their first close encounter with U.S. soldiers. They answered routine questions, but avoided responding when asked directly about insurgents operating in the area. Some families offered the soldiers just-baked bread.

They had completed visiting a set of houses when the patrol leader turned to Cadena, who was the leader of one of the two teams that made up the squad.

"Take us wherever you want to go."

They were on the outskirts of the city now. There were small vegetable plots and vacant fields. The patrol searched an abandoned water treatment plant near the Euphrates River because it looked to Cadena like a good place for an insurgent cache. They found nothing. The men rested for about fifteen minutes so they could drink water and wipe sweat from their eyes.

Cadena looked around and saw a row of houses.

Cadena picked one. The patrol walked up to the house and Cadena knelt down and reached under the front gate to lift the rod that held it closed. Nearly every home has one of these gates and Cadena had done this countless times before. Usually the large metal doors squeak open, giving the occupants warning. This one didn't.

"They just kind of swung open," Cadena recalled. "Good," he thought. "Whoever is inside won't hear us coming."

As Cadena entered the courtyard he noticed the front door was open and that inside were a couple of teenage boys. They were doing something—it wasn't clear what—near the stairs. They looked up, saw a group of American soldiers entering the courtyard, and their eyes widened. With his limited Arabic, Cadena told the boys to stop, hold their hands up, and move toward him. They turned and bolted out the back door. Cadena rushed through the front door.

Spec. Matthew Erickson was right behind Cadena. "Gun!" Erickson yelled.

To Cadena's right a man dressed in a white dishdasha, the traditional loose-fitting robe that many Iraqis wear, was pointing a revolver at Cadena, inches from his head. The man squeezed the trigger, the hammer fell, but the pistol malfunctioned. He fumbled with the pistol, attempting another shot, as Cadena turned rapidly to the right, hitting the man's outstretched arms and knocking him off balance. The sergeant fired six rounds into his chest before the insurgent could regain his balance.

Cadena had seen a man to his left who appeared to be eating some rice and another man to the right of the dead insurgent. Both men had initially put their hands up when Cadena entered the home so the sergeant refrained from firing. Now the man on his left reached for his AK-47.

Cadena fired a couple of rounds at the insurgent but missed. When he turned to the right he saw the other insurgent toss a makeshift grenade out the window.

"Grenade!" Cadena yelled. The entire team, which was still outside the house, hit the ground.

About eight seconds had gone by and Cadena was kicking himself for giving the remaining insurgents time to get out of the house. He figured the grenade was a dud or a fake. Either way, it gave the insurgents time to run. When he lifted his head, he felt the explosion.

"I was like, 'Oh, good, it was a grenade.'"

No one was injured, but by the time the men had gotten up the remaining insurgents had fled over the wall behind the house.

After the team cleared the house to make sure there were no other insurgents or booby traps, one of the soldiers suggested they go back and take a look near where the two teenagers were seen acting oddly. They lifted a tile near the stairs and stared down at a pile of weapons, including two machine guns, two sniper rifles, grenades, and AK-47s. All were wrapped carefully in plastic.

Amid the weapons they made a stunning discovery: a pair of U.S. night vision goggles.

The squad called the serial number on the night vision device back to the company headquarters. A few minutes later the company called back. The goggles were registered to Staff Sgt. Jose Lanzarin, twenty-eight, who had been killed in a roadside bomb attack two days earlier. Lanzarin was a friend of Cadena's.

It's not clear how the sensitive night vision equipment ended up in the house, but Cadena thinks he knows. "We kind of got payback," Cadena said. "I probably shot the guy that killed my buddy."

It was a rare face-to-face confrontation with the enemy. The war in Ramadi, like most of Iraq, was fought at a distance by an enemy who rarely showed himself. Roadside bombs were buried in the street, placed in dead animals, or positioned in storm drains. They were detonated by remote control, using cell phones, garage door openers, or wires. Of the eighty-three Ready First soldiers and marines killed in action in Ramadi, forty-nine deaths were caused by roadside bombs. Another eight were from rockets and mortars. Even when the enemy used rifles, it was usually snipers firing from a distance.

Jason Dickerson was on a patrol when one of their Bradleys ran over a roadside bomb. It did little damage to the heavily armored vehicle, but the soldiers stopped and got out to look around. They found the wire used to detonate the bomb and traced it back to a house on the street. The soldiers entered the abandoned house and found the ends of a wire and battery next to a couch, where the triggermen had been waiting for an American patrol to drive by. There was a half-eaten box of cookies on a table next to the couch. The insurgents had been standing on the couch so they could peer over a wall that surrounded the house and see into the street.

"They were just sitting there, having a snack, waiting for some Americans to come by so they could kill them," Dickerson said. It seemed so ordinary. "It was just as common as you sitting down and having a snack."

Dickerson stared at the couch and the half-eaten cookies. In Ramadi, someone was always watching them.

Ramadi was in some ways worse than MacFarland had expected. It was Iraq's deadliest city, averaging more than twenty attacks per day. Insurgents had free rein in many neighborhoods.

"You own that street for an hour out of the day," a captured insurgent bluntly told dumbfounded U.S. interrogators in Ramadi. "We own it for the other twenty-three. And everyone understands that."

In April, Sterling Jensen, an American interpreter, watched an interrogation of a captured insurgent in Tal Afar. The detainee wouldn't talk, so the American made the detainee stand in the corner and then the interrogator began yelling and kicking chairs in frustration.

"You are afraid of the terrorists more than you are afraid of us!" he screamed.

That was the problem. Few people sympathized with al-Qaeda. Ramadi was almost entirely Sunni and secular in outlook. But people feared al-Qaeda. There was no penalty for not cooperating with the Americans. And the U.S. military, for all its firepower and technology, was not capable of protecting most citizens.

Al-Qaeda all but owned Iraq's most important Sunni city.

4

Back to the Brawl

Let's find out who did it and then we'll kill them.
—MAJ. GEN. JAMES MATTIS, USMC

Maj. Gen. James Mattis was one of the Marine Corps' most innovative officers. He was a vociferous reader of history and literature and was fond of saying "doctrine is the last refuge of the unimaginative." He also developed a reputation as a ruthless foe who embodied the marines' offensive spirit. He would combine both as he arrived in Anbar in 2004 as commander of the First Marine Division. Mattis and his boss, Lt. Gen. James Conway, commander of the First Marine Expeditionary Force, planned on using classic counterinsurgency tactics to protect the population one block at a time. Mattis had helped Gen. David Petraeus in creating the military's new counterinsurgency manual.

In some ways Mattis was a throwback to an earlier century, a romantic figure who saw the nobility of war in addition to its horrors. It was one of the reasons marines loved him. He routinely sprinkled words like "ferocity" and "unmanly" in speeches when other officers talk about exit strategies and metrics.

"We are going back into the brawl," Mattis wrote in a letter to his marines as they readied to deploy overseas in early spring 2004.

But this would be different from a year earlier when the marines were part of the mostly conventional U.S.-led invasion, which broke the back of the Iraqi military and toppled Saddam Hussein's regime. The fight was now against insurgents who hid among the population. This would test the marines and soldiers under his command in new ways. The marines would protect ordinary civilians, but show no quarter to hard-core al-Qaeda militants who would not lay down their arms. Every marine needed the discipline to go from war fighter to diplomat to aid worker within moments. They called it the three-block war. Mattis anticipated the challenge this would pose to nineteen-year-old marines and soldiers.

"The enemy will try to manipulate you into hating all Iraqis," Mattis wrote. "Do not allow the enemy that victory."

Mattis's guidance was simple: "No better friend, no worse enemy." Marines would win friends among the population and destroy those who insist on fighting them.

The words echoed a self-written epitath by Roman general Lucius Cornelius Sulla. It was typical of Mattis, who had studied the ancients. Mattis owned thousands of books, but not a television set. He believed history would provide a "dim light" to help guide his actions in the present. He read literature—including modern fiction—because he knew warfare required an understanding of the human condition as much as weaponry. That was particularly true of an insurgency. For this kind of "war among the population," Mattis said, reading *Angela's Ashes* and Desmond Tutu's writings was as important as military classics by William Sherman and Clausewitz. Understanding the rapprochement in South Africa and Northern Ireland would help cast a light on what the marines needed to do when they returned to Iraq and were placed in charge of Anbar Province.

The Pentagon liked metrics and quantification, but Mattis understood that war among civilians would be won and lost in the human heart. "The indicators that I would consider most significant were, when I walked down the street did people look me in the eye and shake my hand?" Later he noted that one of the Iraqi police stations that didn't break and run when fighting erupted was a tiny outpost that consisted of a half-dozen men in a ramshackle building who shared two weapons among them and had no training or uniforms. It had received poor marks on a U.S. military mandated checklist. The police station that got the highest marks joined the enemy when the fighting got tough. It was hard to measure heart.

"What matters most in war is oftentimes the least easy to measure," Mattis said.

By the time Mattis arrived in Iraq's western desert, it was fast becoming a Hobbesian world of violence and chaos. Sunni insurgents were gaining an upper hand in the main cities of Fallujah and Ramadi. But the "footprint" of U.S. forces was light and the command in Baghdad continued to view Iraq's capital city as the main effort. It was enough to hold off the enemy in

Anbar while U.S. forces worked on securing Baghdad and other major cities.

Mattis thought differently. "We believed that if we could turn Anbar we could set a new tone for the whole war," Mattis said. "We never doubted we could do it." The command in Baghdad saw Anbar as a bastion of Sunnis bitter over the loss of their status, wealth, and power when Saddam's regime collapsed. It would be the last region to be secured. Mattis looked at the same information and saw "reasons why they might be the first to flip."

Sunnis were mostly secular in outlook. The tribal leaders were crafty businesspeople, but they could be reasoned with. There was no reason for the sheiks to throw in their lot with al-Qaeda, but they did so because they were convinced they had no other choice. The Americans would leave and then they would be at the mercy of al-Qaeda, the sheiks figured. Americans hadn't showed them otherwise.

Back at Camp Pendleton, in California, Mattis was studying hard to prepare for the deployment. He had consulted with top Arabists and even the Los Angeles Police Department in helping to train his marines. He had also become convinced that tribes would be the key to unlocking Anbar Province. Tribes "would be the center of our efforts out there from the very beginning," he said.

Less than a week after the marines officially took control of Anbar Province from the Eighty-second Airbone Division, the plan that Mattis and Conway had carefully crafted was derailed.

Mattis was traveling in his new area of operations on March 31 when he received word that CNN was broadcasting a horrific attack on Americans in downtown Fallujah. The marine staff was confused. They didn't have any patrols going through the center of the city. Who were these Americans? What were they doing in the middle of one of Iraq's deadliest cities? Staff officers began to piece it together. Contractors from Blackwater, a security firm, were taking a shortcut through Fallujah while escorting a supply convoy. "Who sent them into Fallujah and why didn't they tell us?" Conway demanded.

The television images were horrific. Within minutes of the ambush a group of men set upon the bodies and the charred remains of two of the men were strung from a bridge over the Euphrates. The images of a rampaging mob defiling American bodies were broadcast around the world.

Conway and Mattis saw no reason to wade into Fallujah. They recovered the bodies—not leaving Americans behind on the battlefield was a matter of no small importance to U.S. Marines—and they began identifying those responsible for the lynching. They would kill or capture the suspects, showing them no quarter. "Okay, just continue what we're doing and do what you can to recover the bodies," Mattis said when learning of the lynching. "Let's find out who did it and then we'll kill them."

That a mob set upon the contractors wasn't all that surprising. "Four white guys in a soft-skinned vehicle could die in a lot of cities in Iraq at that point, and Fallujah was no exception," Conway said.

This was an avoidable mistake, Conway and Mattis figured. It was no reason to derail their counterinsurgency plan.

"I don't want to go into the city," Mattis told Conway.

Conway agreed. It was an easy decision. The marines were as

angered as anybody about the treatment of Americans by an out-of-control mob and the troops were not afraid of a fight. But the commanders closest to the scene knew that punishing the city was a bad idea. An all-out assault on Fallujah would mean civilians would be caught in the middle and the population—the people America needed on its side—would be further alienated. It would mean razing a city they had wanted to win over and tying down thousands of troops that were needed in other parts of the province. They could not react on emotion.

"Once we had Fallujah what were we going to do with it?" Conway thought. "There was no police force. There was no army. So we were going to have to garrison Fallujah and tie down large numbers of troops in a city that would probably be seething and hostile to our presence."

The press made immediate comparisons to Mogadishu, Somalia, when the body of an American soldier was dragged through the streets, an iconic image that was burned in American consciousness. President Bush was among those who saw the images and wanted to know what was going on. Defense Secretary Donald Rumsfeld and the top U.S. administrator in Iraq, Paul Bremer, advocated for an immediate American response.

Conway argued with his higher headquarters in Baghdad, urging them not to overreact. He had clashed in the past with Army Lt. Gen. Ricardo Sanchez, a traditional army officer who advocated a more "kinetic" approach to the war in Iraq. On a previous deployment when the marines had been positioned in the south, Sanchez had insisted they conduct large sweeps through the province or have the army's armored forces do so. What's more, Sanchez (the overall U.S. commander and Conway's boss) made the demands when Conway, who held the same three-star rank as Sanchez, was back in the United States on business. Sanchez traveled south and poked Conway's second-in-command in the chest, attempting to get the marines to change the way they were operating. Conway resented the way Sanchez was trying to "bludgeon" the marines into changing its counter-insurgency approach.

Conway at first thought the order to take Fallujah after the Blackwater killings might have come from Sanchez. If so, Conway would go over his head. He wanted to make sure that the Pentagon knew he objected to an assault on the city. Conway made some discreet inquiries and learned the orders did in fact come from higher than Sanchez. The marines had no choice but to salute and obey.

Mattis's worst fears had materialized. But it was not the nineteen-year-old marines who had failed him. It was the politicians in Washington and the generals in Baghdad who had allowed the militants to goad them into overreacting.

Mattis asked for the orders in writing, which he eventually got, and made another request: "I asked that we [the marines] not be stopped once started," Mattis said.

The marine command quickly drew up plans for an attack into the city. They needed to pull forces from other areas in Anbar, including troublesome areas where insurgents were pressing the attack against U.S. forces.

"We're trying to stick our fingers in all of the holes of the dike," Mattis said. "We don't have enough troops to go around."

The marine command decided to isolate and slowly squeeze

the city, clearing it one neighborhood at a time. They employed lots of snipers, which proved extremely effective in city fighting. The enemy was making mistakes. Large groups of insurgents were gathering at roadblocks and intersections, making it easy for heavily armed AC-130 gunships to target them.

"We've got fifty guys loitering around a roadblock in the middle of town," an AC-130 radioed to the marines. "Do we take them out?" The marines gave them the go-ahead. The gunships, which can fly slow and carry a massive amount of weapons, were extremely effective in this type of fight. At another point an F-16 saw forty or fifty people running out of a mosque toward fighting positions. The marines cleared an air strike, taking out dozens of insurgents with a single bomb. Meanwhile, snipers "owned the streets," Conway said.

The attack was going well. Al-Qaeda's leadership in the city had been decimated and remnants were arguing among themselves. Intercepts indicated they were running out of ammunition. American casualties were light. Six marines had been killed inside the city in the first three days of the offensive.

But, again, the marines would be defeated by images. Al-Jazeera and other Arab satellite news channels were broadcasting video and making claims of heavy civilian casualties. Images of weeping women and children were inflaming the Arab world. Many of the reports were exaggerated or false. The marines acknowledged that there were likely some civilian casualties, but the use of snipers and the methodical pace of the attack had ensured there were few. Many civilians had fled before the offensive started. Commanders suspected that some of the video of injured civilians was file tape taken from some other city. They were furious at the Arab media. "It taught us that these bastards cannot be trusted," Conway said.

The U.S. military denied the allegations, but the reports—combined with images of a major Iraqi city under seige—were setting off alarms across the Arab world. The coalition had established a Governing Council as an interim government after the fall of Saddam's regime. It consisted mostly of formerly exiled Iraqis with almost no base of support in Iraq. Some threatened to resign if the Fallujah fighting wasn't stopped. The British and Italians, meanwhile, were also pressuring the United States to stop the fighting.

Aborting the offensive before it was completed would be worse than launching it in the first place. It would give al-Qaeda a major propaganda victory and hand the militants a sanctuary in the heart of Sunni Anbar Province. Conway was outraged. He told his higher headquarters to hold off.

"We can give you the city in three more days," Conway told them.

His plea was ignored. Marines were ordered to call off the attack and withdraw from the city—only days before securing it. What followed was weeks of fruitless negotiations.

The order may have temporarily placated a handful of Sunni politicians in Baghdad, but it was a costly military and strategic blunder. It gave al-Qaeda a chance to retrain and rearm. Fallujah turned into a forward-operating base for insurgents. They could "go out and launch their attacks and then come back to a secure environment," said U.S. Marine Maj. Gen. Richard F.

Natonski. The withdrawal also handed al-Qaeda an important propaganda victory.

"The second worst thing we could have done was to invade Fallujah," said Marine Maj. Ben Connable, Mattis's cultural adviser. "The worst thing was to leave halfway through. Not only did we throw our counterinsurgency campaign off the rails; we united the population against us, we empowered al-Qaeda, and we proved we could be defeated." Fallujah became a worldwide symbol of Arab resistance to America.

The inevitable came in November when marines attacked the city. The final go-ahead would come from Iraq's newly installed interim prime minister, Ayad Allawi. The night before Allawi was to make his final decision about the attack, U.S. Marine Lt. Gen. John Sattler spoke to the prime minister. Sattler had replaced Conway when his tour was up.

"Mr. Prime Minister, don't tell us to go and expect us to stop," Sattler told Allawi. "Exhaust all political means in an effort to cut a deal, but if a decision is made to assault, don't call it off.

"When you reach that point, just tear your phone out of the wall," Sattler told him. "Don't think about calling us and telling us to stop because once we get going, we're going to have to go all the way."

Allawi agreed.

It was a bloody battle. Insurgents had dug in and fought to the death. Some were high on amphetamines and others had tied off their arms and legs with tourniquets so they could continue to fight if they were shot. The offensive dislodged al-Qaeda from Fallujah and killed more than a thousand militants. Dozens

of Americans were killed in the fighting. It left the city in ruins.
It would take years to rebuild.

Fallujah also gave al-Qaeda a leg up over their nationalist
counterparts in the insurgency. The rebellion that grew out of the
U.S.-led invasion in 2003 was a combination of al-Qaeda—
the hard-core militants who want to establish Islamic rule over
the Arab world—and nationalists, who are mostly secular and
had more limited goals. The nationalists were Sunnis who had
enjoyed power under Saddam and were worried about the rising
influence of Shiites and their Iranian allies. They wanted to get
back in power.

Almost from the outset, American commanders knew that
they should talk to the nationalists and former Baathists. They
were not America's enemies, had some legitimate grievances,
and could be reasoned with. The Fallujah battle now gave America's
enemy the upper hand.

"Fallujah changed the balance, almost like tipping a seesaw,"
Connable said. "The nationalists and Baathists were very strong
up until about April, May, and June 2004. The internal safe haven
of Fallujah gave al-Qaeda in Iraq a springboard."

From the outset the marine command understood that Ramadi
was the key to the province. But the Blackwater fiasco
triggered a series of bad decisions that derailed the marines. Fallujah
became a costly distraction that undercut the marines' plan
to bring Iraq's western desert under control.

"We made Fallujah the center of attention, when in reality
Ramadi should have been the center of attention," Connable
said. "Ramadi was perpetually underresourced."

Even as marines were making the initial attack into Fallujah in 2004, an overwhelmed marine battalion in Ramadi was struggling to protect the government center from being overrun. The marines succeeded, but at a cost. Twelve were killed in one of the bloodiest days for American troops since the U.S.-led invasion.

On the day that the Blackwater contractors were killed, a group of soldiers in Ramadi ran over a roadside bomb while traveling in an armored personnel carrier. It was one of the most powerful roadside bombs encountered to date and killed five soldiers. "All we found was the tailgate and a boot," Conway said. But the television cameras were focused on the mobs in Fallujah.

"We knew Fallujah was a distraction," Connable said. "Ramadi was the key."

5

Fix Ramadi

No great battles awaited Alexander; he was to be
faced by a people's war, a war of mounted guerrillas
who, when he advanced would suddenly appear in
his rear, who entrenched themselves on inaccessible
crags, and when pursued vanished into the Turkoman
steppes.

—J.F.C. FULLER

It was a tradition for most brigades in Iraq to place photos of
the fallen soldiers on the walls of headquarters. It was a way to
honor the men and women who had died in battle. The faces of
the dead would stare out at the living; a silent reminder of the cost
of war. The neat line of framed pictures would grow with time.

When MacFarland got orders to take his brigade to Ramadi
he knew it would amount to a "death sentence" for many of his
soldiers. "We had all heard the stories about Ramadi," he said.

MacFarland ordered that the photos of the dead be taken

from his headquarters and placed in the chapel. Officers are taught from the time they pin on their second lieutenant's gold bars that their twin responsibilities are to take care of their soldiers and accomplish the mission. They also learn that the lives of their soldiers—the men and women in their charge—must sometimes take a backseat to taking the hill.

MacFarland had read *Death of a Division*, the story of one of the worst setbacks in World War II. Two regiments of the 106th Division, a young, untested unit, surrendered to the Germans at the Battle of the Bulge. What stuck in his mind was that one of the regimental command posts was established alongside the field hospital as the battle with the Germans raged. The dead and wounded were stacking up in plain view of the colonel directing the fight. He could see only the human cost of the fight, blinding him to the mission. He surrendered his regiment to the Germans. If your only goal is to protect your troops, victory will be impossible.

MacFarland ordered the photos moved to the chapel. "I went to every memorial service. I went to every hero flight. I went to Charlie Med [the field hospital] whenever I could and whenever a seriously wounded soldier or marine came in there.

"But I didn't want to look at those faces every single time to be reminded of the human cost."

The battles in Fallujah had sidetracked the command in western Iraq, but now—two years later—it was time to focus on the most important city in Anbar Province. "Our focus coming out here was to zero in on Ramadi," said Zilmer, who arrived in 2006.

In the spring, shortly after his headquarters arrived in Anbar, Zilmer ordered his staff to come up with a plan for Ramadi. They put together a team of the smartest minds on the staff to figure out how to take the city back. The plan would be sent to higher headquarters in Baghdad, so the marine officers knew they couldn't ask for the sky. "We understood that despite the fact that the Department of Defense was making public proclamations to the effect that commanders would get whatever they asked for, we knew that it would be in our best interest to ask for the bare minimum that we actually needed," said Maj. Ben Connable, an intelligence analyst who helped draft the plan. They figured that way they would get what they needed.

They developed a plan, which included building outposts, and asked for more troops than were currently in the city. They wanted the troops to arrive well before the current National Guard unit in Ramadi was to leave. That way there would be a temporary surge of forces when both units were in the city.

The plan went first to Lt. Gen. Peter Chiarelli, commander of Multi-National Corps–Iraq, who told the marines he was skeptical they would get what they asked for, but passed the request to Gen. George Casey, the top commander in Iraq. Casey believed that it was the presence of U.S. troops that was fueling much of the violence.

"What came back down is, you'll get a lot less than you asked for and it won't fit your timeline," Connable said.

"Up to that point most of us bought into that whole line that commanders get what they ask for.

"That was a blatant lie."

Connable was stunned. Ramadi was turning into an insurgent

stronghold every bit as bad as Fallujah had been. The U.S. military had taken to firing satellite-guided rockets, bombs, and artillery into downtown Ramadi. The city was turning to rubble. One day, Connable walked into the combat operations center at Camp Fallujah to find the fire support officer jumping for joy because it had been the first time a new satellite-guided rocket system had been fired in combat. Connable just shook his head. "These guys just didn't get how far things had fallen apart, how low we had sunk in terms of security."

Casey's staff eventually agreed to send the First Brigade, First Armored Division to Ramadi. It had fewer soldiers than the marines had asked for and they were skeptical of sending a heavy armored unit with tanks into a city. The marines were more inclined to go with light infantry. The turnover with the outgoing unit would not be long enough to create the temporary surge that the marine command had hoped for.

MacFarland's orders when he arrived in Anbar were simple: "Fix Ramadi but don't do a Fallujah."

The colonel was a little surprised he wasn't given more direction, particularly since holding Ramadi was so important to the insurgents. The insurgents boasted that Ramadi was the capital of the caliphate that al-Qaeda planned on establishing across the Islamic world. They regularly issued propaganda videos from their sanctuaries inside the city.

"I wasn't really quite sure how I was going to fix Ramadi," he said.

The commander of the First Marine Expeditionary Force,

Maj. Gen. Richard Zilmer, had a reputation of giving his subordinates a lot of latitude. It made sense in a counterinsurgency fight. Each area of Iraq differed. Even within Anbar Province, which was at least 90 percent Sunni, there were differences. Fallujah was a religious enclave where imams held sway. Ramadi, the seat of government, was more secular. Outside the city was farmland where sheiks still wielded influence. What worked in one place might not in another.

There wasn't a lot of direction coming from Baghdad and Washington, other than the guidance to turn responsibility over to the Iraqis as soon as possible so U.S. troops could come home. The strategy wasn't working, but no one had come up with a better idea. The war was losing support day by day and President Bush's polls were sinking.

There was an increasing sense of doom seizing Washington and parts of the U.S. command in Baghdad. The Ready First was rolling into Ramadi as sectarian violence in Baghdad was escalating in the wake of al-Qaeda's bombing of the Golden Mosque in Samarra in February. It was an important Shiite shrine and the attack touched off a wave of Sunni-Shiite warfare that raged through Baghdad neighborhoods. Efforts to quell the violence and take the initiative from the insurgents were failing.

There was an entrepreneurial bent to this war as colonels, and even captains, fought the war in their own ways, with varying results.

MacFarland's plans were predicated on the assumption his force would shrink as the tour wore on. "Ours will be a strategy of limited means," MacFarland told his staff one week after arriving.

And they would have to move fast. "I've got to strike while I had the combat power with me," MacFarland thought. MacFarland's brigade was initially sent to Tal Afar in northern Iraq, arriving in January 2006 to replace a brigade that was hailed as the first major counterinsurgency success story in Iraq. The brigade commander there, Col. H. R. MacMasters, had successfully put together a strategy that combined working with sheiks and setting up combat outposts inside the city to protect civilians.

MacFarland and his staff absorbed the lessons of MacMaster's Third Armored Cavalry Regiment, but Ramadi would be a tougher nut to crack. Ramadi was more important politically because it was a major city in the center of Iraq's Sunni population. That meant it was also at the core of Iraq's growing insurgency. Unlike Tal Afar, cracking the problem in Ramadi had the potential to change the course of the war.

Before the Ready First arrived in Ramadi, a National Guard brigade had been in the city for a year. It had secured the main avenue through Ramadi and the major east-west supply route that traversed its area between the Syrian border and Baghdad. Toward the end of the tour the National Guard unit had also set up some static checkpoints in an effort to isolate the city.

The main supply routes were secure, but insurgents had a free rein over many other parts of the city. There were "no-go" areas that U.S. forces avoided, leaving al-Qaeda free to terrorize neighborhoods and plot attacks. There was little U.S. presence in the center of the city, aside from a battalion of marines. A battalion of army paratroopers were positioned on the east side of the city at Camp Corregidor. Much of the brigade remained primarily on the large bases and commuted into the city.

"They were treading water," said Lt. Col. Pete Lee, MacFarland's executive officer.

The U.S. military likes to say that part-time soldiers have the same capabilities as their active-duty counterparts. But National Guard soldiers train one weekend per month, compared to the rigorous round-the-clock training that active units undergo. The Guard soldiers are often older and have skill sets that active-duty units don't have. Guardsmen are cops, lawyers, and businessmen. Those are great skills to bring to a nation-building mission.

In 2005, however, Ramadi was a toe-to-toe fight between al-Qaeda and the U.S. military. The National Guard unit was not the best outfit to slug it out with al-Qaeda for control of the city.

The National Guard was dispatched to Ramadi in 2005 at a time when the Pentagon was struggling to get enough troops to Iraq for a war that wasn't supposed to last this long.

The Second Brigade, Twenty-eighth Infantry Division was pieced together from units in more than ten states. Individual soldiers came from more than thirty states. The brigade trained together at Camp Shelby in Mississippi and Fort Irwin, California, for about five months before deploying to Iraq. Then they were sent to Iraq's deadliest city.

"We were building the brigade mostly as we were training," said Col. John Gronski, the brigade commander.

"This whole issue with these elements coming together wasn't ideal, but we never complained about it and we did what we had to do to train and get up to speed," Gronski said.

Marine Maj. Teddy Gates, a reservist who was a cop in Virginia in civilian life, arrived in Ramadi in February 2006 to work with the National Guard to help recruit and train police. He was surprised to find some of the guardsmen were old enough to have served in Vietnam. In April, Gates was helping with a police recruiting drive at a U.S. base along the Euphrates River when insurgents began firing on the Americans from a building across the street.

Rain was pouring down and Gates was huddled in a small sandbagged position with the guardsmen. As the Americans fired back, the insurgents' shooting would die down. "And then as we'd back off to see what would happen, they'd come back," Gates said. Gates was puzzled. *Why can't they hit the insurgents and end this firefight?* The militants would keep bouncing back despite a heavy volume of U.S. firepower. The shooting went on like this for about forty-five minutes.

There was a growing cloud of dust inside the bunker. "The more we'd fight, the more this dust increased." Gates looked over at a staff sergeant, who also appeared old enough to have served in Vietnam. He noticed that he wore eyeglasses as thick as Coke bottles.

"Every time he'd shoot, he's hitting the top of the sandbag."

The National Guard brigade was also not equipped and organized to meet the challenges in Ramadi. The unit had about the same number of soldiers, about 5,400, as MacFarland's brigade, but they didn't have as many tanks and armor. They also had a larger area that they were responsible for.

"Col. Gronski did the best he could, but the unit didn't have the resources and was not properly matched to the mission," Gates said.

"In an urban setting having a heck of a lot of armor is a huge advantage. You don't want it to be a fair fight. You want to bring a gun to a knife fight."

The brigade fought hard and took losses. They did everything that was asked of them. They lost eighty-two soldiers and marines to combat during their yearlong deployment. They were attacked by one thousand roadside bombs. About another thousand were discovered before they were detonated.

"These are Pennsylvania coal miners and good 'ole boys from Appalachia and they were duking it out and they were holding their own," said Col. Pete Devlin, the top intelligence officer in Anbar.

Gronski said they lacked enough forces to hold the entire city. "I made a conscious decision to never order units into an area we had never been to for months and months" unless they were prepared to clear and hold the area, he said. Gronski said insurgents had seeded roadside bombs througout the city to prevent U.S. forces from entering particular areas. But he said they were still able to clear and hold neighborhoods that had been insurgent safe havens.

"The fault lies with whoever sent Two Twenty-eight to Ramadi," said Lt. Col. Jim Lechner, MacFarland's blunt-talking deputy commander.

"That's the most assinine decision I've ever heard of."

Lt. Col. Ronald Clark's battalion, the First of the 506th Infantry Regiment, arrived at Corregidor at about 2 A.M. one day in November 2005, while the National Guard was still in charge. At about 6 A.M. Clark was awakened by an air raid siren. A small barrage of seven 130mm rockets landed in the camp. The battalion they had replaced had lost six soldiers to mortar and rocket fire *inside* the compound during the preceding six months. At Corregidor soldiers had to wear their protective gear to go to the chow hall or the latrine. Later, Clark was sitting in the tactical operations center with the commander and operations officer of the battalion his unit was replacing. They heard a large explosion. No siren sounded.

"What was that?" Clark asked.

Probably a rocket-propelled grenade, he was told.

Clark was dumbfounded. The maximum effective range of an RPG is about three hundred meters. *Insurgents are operating that close to the base.*

Clark turned to his operations officer. "That is unacceptable."

Clark's unit was an active-duty battalion that was under the command of the National Guard when they first arrived in November 2005. They would remain after the Ready First arrived in the spring of 2006.

Clark was amazed at the brazenness of the enemy when he arrived in Ramadi. "These guys are too bold," Clark told his operations officer and executive officer. He decided to test them.

They started a "call to fight." First, they would select an area where they wanted to fight. Then they would place soldiers and snipers around the area to seal it off. They sent out their psychological operations teams with a message they read in Arabic over loudspeakers as they drove through a neighborhood: "Those insurgents among you who choose to come out and fight, if you're truly brave, if you're true to your calling, stop hiding behind women and children and come out and fight us."

Drones buzzing overhead would relay what happened next. Insurgents would broadcast their own message from loudspeakers attached to a minaret at the local mosque, telling their people to gather at the mosque. The Americans would watch from their command post as men rallied for the chance to fight Americans.

"They'd put on their black masks and gun up and come out and fight," Clark said.

As MacFarland and his staff began planning for their campaign in Ramadi, Abu Musab al-Zarqawi, the Jordanian-born head of al-Qaeda in Iraq, was killed June 8, 2006, by an American air strike north of Baghdad. Zilmer told MacFarland four days later that he wanted him to speed up the brigade's plan to take back the center of the city. The plan was to take advantage of any dissension and confusion among insurgents in the wake of Zarqawi's death.

It turned out there wasn't much confusion in the ranks as a result of Zarqawi's death. The U.S. command consistently misread the importance of hierarchy in the insurgency. Much of it was decentralized and run by local captains.

Within weeks of arriving, the brigade built four combat outposts—Iron, Spear, Eagle's Nest, and Falcon in southern Ramadi. They were complicated operations involving setting up security using Navy SEAL snipers and conventional forces and then rushing in engineers with cranes and other troops to quickly establish fortified positions with every manner of concrete barrier. They used tons of sandbags. Every soldier at Camp Ramadi had to fill a sandbag before he went into the chow hall. The new combat outposts, called COPs, would be manned by U.S. soldiers and whatever Iraqi forces they could muster. They got so quick at the process of establishing the outposts they called them COPs in a Box.

Insurgents woke up to find Americans in their backyard.

MacFarland wanted to take the initiative away from the enemy, who had the luxury of attacking when and where they wanted. One of the most effective weapons against insurgents was snipers. They generally didn't cause collateral damage and they wore at the morale of insurgents. Snipers fanned out into the city. The psychological impact was profound.

"You never know where a sniper round is coming from," MacFarland said.

Interrogations and other types of intelligence showed that insurgents had become terrified of snipers. "They began to attribute almost any bad thing that happened to them to snipers, even when we had no one in the area," he said.

The new soldiers were coming under attack by roadside bombs and snipers, but it was not the intense opposition that they had expected.

The Ready First had caught a break. The enemy misread MacFarland's intentions.

In May, its tanks and armor lumbered into Ramadi. The

brigade brought seventy-seven tanks and eighty-four Bradleys, along with hundreds of armored Humvees.

The brigade was part of the storied First Armored Division, "Old Ironsides," which blunted Rommel's advance in North Africa. It wasn't one of the new "modular brigades," the sleek combat units that can be "task-organized" and quickly mobilized for any fight. It was a "legacy" brigade, a holdover from the old army. The brigade was a cold war relic designed to hold off the Soviet army at the Fulda Gap. During the Persian Gulf War, it led the sweeping left hook that broke what remained of Saddam's army.

The sudden influx of American forces and armor convinced people in Ramadi that the U.S. military was about to launch another Fallujah-style campaign. Families packed into cars were fleeing the city. Soldiers asked them why. "We hear they're going to clear it like Fallujah," the soldiers were told. "We're outta here." Al-Qaeda was leaving too. "They basically vacated their strongholds in the center of the city," says Lt. Col. Ronald Clark, who commanded a battalion in eastern Ramadi. The Fallujah offensive had dealt a blow to the insurgents and they didn't want a repeat.

"They thought we were going to level the place," said Maj. Eric Remoy, the brigade's intelligence officer.

The U.S. media picked up on the rumors. A headline in the *Los Angeles Times* blared, FEAR OF BIG BATTLE PANICS IRAQI CITY. No such battle was planned, but the U.S. military did nothing to correct the misimpression.

The enemy was laying low and it was unnerving. "The enemy is almost too quiet," MacFarland thought.

He started trying to figure out how to exploit the opening.

They continued to build outposts in the worst parts of the city, in neighborhoods that al-Qaeda had controlled.

"Sooner or later they will realize that their caution has been turned against them and they will have lost freedom of maneuver in Ramadi," MacFarland figured.

It wouldn't be long before al-Qaeda realized its mistake.

6

Falcon

Wars may be fought with weapons, but they are won by men.

—GEN. GEORGE PATTON

"You guys are going to get a lot of people killed," a National Guard civil affairs officer warned Sterling Jensen, an American translator assigned to the Ready First. "You guys are really arrogant."

MacFarland's brigade replaced the National Guard unit in late May. As part of the transition the outgoing unit worked for a couple of weeks with the new people.

National Guard officers warned the soldiers of the Ready First that there were parts of the city that were off-limits. Some roads were seeded with roadside bombs and they were almost certain to take casualties on them. Even the marine battalion that was in the heart of the city warned the brigade.

Anything south of Route Michigan, which ran through the

center of the city, was "Indian country," they said. "If you go in there you're going to lose soldiers and you're going to get killed," Capt. Mike Bajema was warned.

The Ready First made no secret of the fact they planned a different approach. They would go into Indian country—with tanks if necessary. They wouldn't cede an inch of territory to the enemy.

MacFarland's staff quickly drew up plans for troops to move straight into the heart of insurgent safe havens. Already, Ready First soldiers were rolling along Route Michigan, the street that went through the heart of the city. They were regularly coming under attack with roadside bombs or from insurgents darting out of alleys with rocket-propelled grenades. Every day, his soldiers were under attack. About a week after arriving MacFarland's convoy of three Humvees along with two tanks were driving west on Route Michigan when an insurgent in an alley on their right fired at the vehicles. The grenade passed between his Humvee and the one in front of him. They never saw who fired it and kept moving. MacFarland decided that his personal security detail was going to have to up its game if he was to survive this tour.

The heavy tanks and armored vehicles were magnets for insurgents, which worried some marine officers, who favored foot patrols and less intrusive actions. "They're huge targets," Maj. Ben Connable, the intelligence officer, said. "Every time you lose a tank it's a tremendous propaganda victory for the enemy. It's easy to take a picture of a blown-up tank and it looks great because tanks are supposed to be invulnerable.

"They intimidate the population. The last thing you want to do is intimidate the population."

Part of the disagreement over tactics reflected the difference between the way infantry and armored units approached the fight. The marines—essentially light infantry—were moving at night in small teams, doing census and other operations. They had four tanks in the city and only brought them out when they wanted to make a big statement.

"Up front we pointed out that aggressive heavy-handed tactics typically don't work," a marine officer said. He said the brigade ignored their advice, even though the marine unit, Third Battalion, Eighth Marines, had been there for about five months when the Ready First arrived. "They were very blasé about some of the things we warned them about."

The armor officers argued the tank was misunderstood. Its 120mm main gun round was ideal for blowing a hole in a cinder block wall without bringing down the entire building. And they said they were fighting in parts of the city where there were few civilians.

The Third Infantry Division's famed Thunder Run into Baghdad during the 2003 invasion proved the worth of tanks in the urban battlefield, Lt. Col. V. J. Tedesco figured. "That completely pulled the shroud away from the school of thought that tanks have no place in urban warfare," said Tedesco, commander of 1-37 Armor.

MacFarland put Tedesco, one of his most aggressive commanders, near the heart of the city, poised to attack into the most dangerous areas and set up small outposts. His battalion ended up firing about a hundred main gun rounds during their time in Ramadi. The battalion lost twenty-five tanks, Bradley Fighting Vehicles, and trucks to roadside bombs. "We just absorbed IEDs," Tedesco said, referring to improvised explosive devices.

Capt. Mike Bajema, one of Tedesco's company commanders, was assigned the job of establishing Falcon, the first major outpost inside the city. They decided to build the outpost in a few homes in south-central Ramadi that straddled key routes through the city.

But when Bajema went out at night to scout the location, he decided it was too small. He planned on bringing his entire company, plus support personnel, which was about two hundred men. Plus, there needed to be room for Iraqi soldiers. Instead of three houses he would need about seven. Most were occupied by Iraqi families. The plan was to have the Iraqi Army eject them from their houses. The Iraqis refused; they didn't want to anger the locals.

The marines were horrified at the tactics. "They gave the residents about thirty minutes to get their stuff out," one officer said. "It created a lot of ill will."

But the brigade was determined to establish a foothold in the city. They gave each of seven families $2,500 a month for their homes and ordered them out.

Now they had to launch a complex operation to build a fortified base and move a couple hundred American soldiers inside enemy territory—all inside twenty-four hours. They launched the operation before dawn, positioning U.S. Navy SEAL snipers and a sister company to secure the surrounding area. They placed snipers on rooftops and secured key intersections. Engineers set to work putting up blast walls, hooking up generators, and building guard towers. The frenzied work was done by soldiers wearing full combat gear in temperatures that exceeded a hundred degrees. By midmorning the enemy was already fighting back, apparently surprised by the brazen move into its backyard. Insurgents fired three 120mm mortar rounds at the new outpost, killing Spec. Terry Lisk, twenty-six, and injuring another five or six soldiers. The soldiers kept building.

For the next three days trucks moved back and forth between the new outpost and Camp Ramadi, bringing more than a hundred sections of concrete wall and 50,000 sandbags. They kept improving the fortifications over the next couple of weeks. Most of the time they were under fire. But within two weeks the outpost was impenetrable with .50 caliber machine guns on the roof and interlocking fields of fire. Tedesco told Bajema to start patrolling.

Bajema's men began clearing the neighborhood, block by block. Bajema's company was aggressive. "If a door was locked we wouldn't just say, 'Well, no one is home. Let's keep going,'" Bajema says. "First, we would try and knock. If knocking didn't work we would try and bash the door in with a battering ram. And if that didn't work, I would use C-4 [explosives] and blow the side of the house up."

This was not a hearts-and-minds approach. They wanted to kick the enemy in the teeth. Bajema's tactics raised eyebrows. "Some of the other company commanders looked at that type of aggressiveness and they were concerned that blowing up the side of a house to gain entry is only going to cause the people to turn against our actions," Bajema said. "We came out there to root out the enemy." Bajema said it was necessary to get the enemy's attention and also convince the locals that they were dead serious about going after the insurgents.

Bajema was supposed to go in with Iraqi security forces. There was no sense in just creating American outposts. His company was working with an Iraqi battalion that had been moved from northern Iraq to Ramadi, as part of a small surge of forces into Ramadi. When the Iraqi battalion received orders to Ramadi, about 80 percent of the soldiers turned in their paperwork and quit. The remnants of the battalion, mostly officers, rolled into Ramadi a few days later.

It didn't get any better when they arrived. On July 2, one of their convoys hit a small roadside bomb on their way to Combat Outpost Falcon. Two soldiers from the Second Iraqi Division received minor injuries and their U.S.-supplied Humvee sustained flat tires. When the rest of the battalion learned of the attack, the entire unit demanded to leave Ramadi or they would quit.

Once at Falcon, they refused to go out on a joint patrol with the Americans, convinced that they would be targets. They went out twice on their own and both times had soldiers killed, refusing to go out and retrieve the bodies. Bajema was furious. He had to retrieve the bodies for a unit that refused to patrol with his soldiers.

In less than two weeks MacFarland had already lost ten of his soldiers in Ramadi and had no patience for an Iraqi unit that wouldn't fight. He didn't want their attitude to infect other Iraqi army units in Anbar that were fighting alongside Americans. They were put on trucks, sent back to Baghdad, replaced by an

Iraqi army unit from Baghdad, which performed well. At the time the quality of Iraqi forces varied widely.

By early August, Bajema's men had pushed the insurgents out of most neighborhoods around Falcon, but there were a couple of areas that had yet to be secured. The Navy SEALs had received intelligence about two homes that housed insurgents and were functioning as an al-Qaeda headquarters. They were near a mosque that had used the loudspeaker on its minaret as a way of rallying insurgents. The buildings were located only five blocks from Falcon, within small arms range.

They didn't have exact locations of the houses. "We knew what block they were on and that was the best the informant could do," Bajema said.

On August 2 they launched a company-sized operation along with the SEALs to sweep through the neighborhood from east to west. The tanks and armored Bradleys rolled into the neighborhood before first light. Men were on the streets going to morning prayers. The insurgents were waiting. They let the armor pass and opened up on the infantry, who came in next. They fired from alleys, buildings, and around every corner. Almost immediately a Navy SEAL, Ryan Job, was hit. A sniper round hit the top of his light machine gun, sending shards of hot metal into his face and eyes, blinding him. A corpsman ran to him and began treating his wound, as other SEALs intentionally exposed themselves to enemy bullets in order to draw fire away from their wounded comrade. The Americans identified where the sniper round had come from. Two tanks swiveled their turrets and fired three rounds each, destroying the building. That stopped the insurgents, at least temporarily.

The neighborhood was crawling with well-concealed enemy snipers and insurgents hidden amid vacant buildings and shadowy alleys. It's likely the past several weeks of operations inside the enemy stronghold of south-central Ramadi had pushed the insurgents into a corner and they were going to fight back hard. Bajema's men had stumbled on a much larger force than he anticipated. There were probably fifty insurgents darting between buildings and alleyways, raining fire on his force.

Bajema decided to withdraw his forces and try again at night, when the advantage would go to Americans with night vision goggles. A Bradley Fighting Vehicle was called in, rushing through the rubble-strewn streets to evacuate Job. Bajema's men sealed the neighborhood with tanks and Bradleys as they withdrew forces so the enemy couldn't leave or be reinforced.

Bajema's tank was the last one to leave. Without warning the enemy came out in force, emerging from alleys, buildings, and behind corners. He found himself surrounded on four sides by an enemy armed with rocket-propelled grenades, machine guns, and rifles. Bajema was blasting back with his tank's machine guns and main gun, killing a couple dozen insurgents. Bajema radioed into his battalion headquarters to tell them he was heavily engaged with the enemy.

"Mike, what's going on?" the battalion's executive officer asked Bajema. "What do you need to keep killing these sons of bitches?" They decided Bajema would stay in the fight.

Once a commander declares "troops in contact," the battalion provides him with video feeds from surveillance aircraft, artillery, and other assets. For the first time that day, Bajema had a look at where the insurgents were and what weapons they were carrying. Video from an orbiting drone above the fight showed a group of men jumping into a car on a side street and preparing to flee. It was happening only a few blocks away.

Bajema's tank continued to blast away with its main gun and machine gun, as he worked his way over to where the drone had seen insurgents piling into the car. He got there just as the insurgents were about to take off. Insurgents were leaning out of the windows firing their AK-47s futilely at the tank. Bajema's tank opened fire with its coaxial machine guns, destroying the vehicle and killing the men inside.

The SEALs, meanwhile, had returned to Falcon for more ammunition. They loaded into Bradleys and came out to where Bajema was in contact with the enemy. A SEAL had been badly injured and they wanted back in the fight. They had asked for the army to take them back into the city in their Bradleys.

The Navy SEALs had developed unusually close bonds with Bajema's soldiers. The SEALs wore army uniforms and began to refer to themselves as "Army SEALs." That wasn't typical for an elite unit that often operates by a set of rules different from those of its conventional counterparts. But the soldiers and SEALs lived and fought together in one of Ramadi's toughest neighborhoods and had come to rely on one another.

Bajema's tank was holding off the insurgents, who had begun regrouping into two buildings. Bajema used the front of his tank to smash down the outer wall of the compound, and a main gun round blasted a hole in the side of the house. The SEALs rushed into one of the buildings and began clearing it. Petty Officer

Second Class Marc Lee, twenty-eight, exposed himself in a window and began firing at the enemy with his small machine gun. He was shot in the face by the enemy and died instantly. The SEALs managed to kill eight insurgents in the building.

The battle outside the building was just as intense. Insurgents opened up on the armored Bradleys that had brought the SEALs in. Bajema had run out of tank ammunition and so the Bradleys fired their 25mm chain gun and TOW 2 anti-tank missiles that are mounted on the heavily armored vehicles.

The fighting began at 5 A.M. and wasn't over until about 4 P.M.

The firefight had brought the full range of American firepower into downtown Ramadi and bodies were buried under piles of rubble. They had used more than 10,000 machine gun rounds, over 3,000 rounds from the 25mm Bradley chain gun, called in several air strikes, and fired more than twenty main gun rounds from their tanks.

"We had caused a lot of damage destroying the enemy," Bajema said. Job had lost his sight and Lee had been killed, the first Navy SEAL to die in Iraq. Most of the other U.S. injuries were light shrapnel wounds. Bajema figured they killed about forty insurgents, but it was hard to be certain.

The exhausted soldiers rolled back into Falcon in the late afternoon. They had been fighting for about twelve hours in 120-degree heat.

MacFarland was usually on his doorstep before the smoke cleared from a pitched battle, asking about how to improve a neighborhood once it was cleared of insurgents. Typically, Bajema would excitedly give MacFarland a breathless play-by-play from a recent battle.

"Good job. Now how are you going to fix it?" MacFarland said.

"Mike, I need you to go back into that neighborhood tomorrow and find out what they need from us, whether that's food, sugar, heating oil."

"Two hours after being in a gun battle with the enemy I'm not really thinking about" providing essential services to a neighborhood, Bajema said.

Bajema's men fought hard in stifling heat throughout the summer. The company commander was slim to begin with and he had lost about fifteen pounds by late July. On a visit to Falcon, MacFarland was alarmed. He ordered Bajema to take better care of himself and told Tedesco, the battalion commander, to keep an eye on him. Tedesco later ordered him to take his two-week leave. Bajema had planned to take his leave after all his troops had already taken theirs.

"The choice is not yours," Tedesco said.

A marine battalion held downtown Ramadi, the most violent part of Iraq's deadliest city. Militants moved freely through rubble-strewn streets and had built fighting positions in abandoned buildings, some of which were booby-trapped to blow up if they were entered by coalition forces. There were more than a hundred suspected roadside bombs in the marines' three-kilometer area of operations on any given day. Every day the government center came under attack.

Even as Sattar and his tribes began securing the outskirts of the city, downtown remained a no-man's-land.

On September 21, the day that Capt. Jayson Arthaud's company officially took responsibility for securing the government center, his marines came under a sustained assault that was triggered by a truck bomb detonated at a checkpoint a half block west of the building. It knocked down a small building, consuming it in flames. About fifty insurgents organized into small squads were maneuvering toward the building from all sides. The marines at the checkpoint called for the quick reaction force, worried that they were surrounded. Arthaud denied it. The squad, about a dozen marines, had ammunition and no serious casualties and were still fighting. The quick reaction force might be needed elsewhere. "Just keep fighting," Arthaud told them.

Arthaud's men responded with machine-gun and rifle fire. Marines ran upstairs to the roof of the government center, lugging ammunition to supply marksmen firing at insurgents who were dashing across streets and trying to make their way to the marine position. After a two-and-a-half-hour firefight, the marines had expended between five thousand and eight thousand rounds of ammunition, fighting in temperatures that were well over a hundred degrees. Only one marine was injured in the attack and dozens of insurgents were killed, but al-Qaeda made a point: They would fight for Ramadi.

"That was the first play of the game," said Marine Lt. Col. Bill Jurney, commander of First Battalion, Sixth Marines.

"I hope every day is not going to be like this," Arthaud thought when it was over.

The marines, whose history is steeped in counterinsurgency or "small wars," planned on establishing outposts in their area. Jurney had come to Ramadi prepared to use classic counterinsurgency tactics, having his marines live among the population and develop a close relationship with the Iraqi army and police.

He was surprised to find MacFarland, commander of an armored force designed to take on the Soviets, thought the same way. "He's not going to tell you how to skin the cat, but he gave very clear guidance on what he needed us to do," Jurney said. "I couldn't have been happier when I saw his methods of employment, which is not what I expected from an armored officer in the army."

Shortly after taking over in September, Jurney ordered his men to build a permanent position in the 17th Street area, a circular street near the government center. The military called it the Racetrack. It had once been home to thriving markets and storefronts, which were now abandoned. It was the worst of the worst. Insurgents roamed freely in the area and had set up a shadow government.

The marines killed nineteen insurgents on the day they seized the outpost, but insurgents fought back hard. The outpost at the Racetrack received 85 percent of the mortar and rocket fire brought to bear on the brigade during the first two weeks it was established.

"That was a significant emotional event for the enemy," Jurney said. "He knew we weren't leaving. Now we were hunting him."

7

Counterattack

Those days we lived in hell. We looked like ghosts
out of a cemetery.

—WIFE OF A POLICEMAN IN ANBAR
DESCRIBING LIFE UNDER AL-QAEDA

From the rubble of downtown Ramadi, insurgents have a clear view of the hospital on the edge of town. They can track American convoys as they leave the hospital grounds and watch to see if they head for the center of Ramadi.

It was early afternoon on July 24 when the small four-vehicle convoy left Ramadi Hospital where Lt. Col. Jim Lechner, Mac-Farland's deputy commander, had checked on a small police contingent there. Capt. Jason West, a young staff officer who was part of a team that handled administrative issues for the Iraqi police, accompanied him. Lechner's convoy took a right at the Saddam Mosque and entered Route Michigan, the street that goes through the heart of downtown Ramadi. The small convoy rolled past pockmarked buildings and piles of rubble as it headed downtown.

It had been a difficult few weeks in Ramadi. The Ready First had established its initial combat outposts and the enemy, after an initial lull, had begun to fight back. A week earlier, Mac-Farland had escaped unscathed after a roadside bomb detonated under his vehicle on Route Michigan after visiting the hospital. On the same day, one of his tanks hit a small roadside bomb that caused a fuel cell to burst into flames. It was hours before they could retrieve the body of the tank commander who was killed after he got out and stepped on another roadside bomb. The tank was burning and the ammunition was "cooking off."

Lechner's small convoy rolled up to an intersection not far from the government center in downtown Ramadi. Lechner is a fireplug of a man and an aggressive officer who is restless sitting behind a desk. Lechner had his convoy execute a "slingshot" maneuver. The two lead Humvees drove up to the intersection, defending the position so the rear vehicles could drive through. The lead Humvees would then follow and repeat the tactic at the next intersection. West was in one of the two lead Humvees and Lechner was right behind them.

The insurgents triggered the ambush almost as soon as the vehicles arrived at the intersection. When they saw the Americans heading their way, the insurgents probably used poles to slide a roadside bomb into the streets. Down several dark alleyways they had set up 57mm rockets on homemade launchers. They hunkered down and waited.

The insurgents detonated the roadside bombs in front of the

lead vehicles. Insurgents then triggered the ambush, shooting at the vehicles from covered positions amid the rubble. To get out of the kill zone, the convoy began to roll. More roadside bombs began detonating in front of them as they rolled out of the kill zone. Insurgents started firing rockets from the alleyways. One hit West's Humvee, killing the twenty-eight-year-old officer instantly.

The convoy raced through the barrage of fire and got to the safety of the government center, which was several blocks away and protected by a company of marines. Sterling Jensen looked in front of his Humvee and saw some soldiers carrying a body out of a Humvee. His leg was twisted at an unnatural angle.

"We have lost a guy," Jensen thought.

Later he got out of the vehicle and escorted a wounded soldier in his Humvee to the aid station in the government center. On his way back to the Humvee, Jensen saw the marines bring in a body on a strecher. Jensen stared at his face for several seconds before recognizing it was West. He noticed a gold cross on a chain around his neck.

At the tactical operations center, staff officers were monitoring the radios when the report came that Lechner's convoy was ambushed and they had a KIA, a soldier killed in action. The operations center, normally buzzing with activity, fell silent. Only the radios continued to crackle in the background.

The staff had to wait twenty minutes before a name was reported. "It's West."

The ambush on Route Michigan was one of twenty-four attacks in a thirty-minute period across Ramadi on that day. The attacks were launched by about a hundred fighters. The brigade had received intelligence reports that Abu Musab al-Zarqawi's replacement as head of al-Qaeda in Iraq, Abu Ayoub al-Masri, held a meeting in a date palm grove around Ramadi shortly before the attack. Intelligence officers figured he probably was in the city planning the assault. West and a soldier in eastern Ramadi were killed that day. The Americans killed about thirty insurgents during the clashes.

Al-Qaeda recognized things were not going well for it in Ramadi. They didn't want to lose their sanctuary. The combat outposts that the Ready First had established posed a threat to one of its most important sanctuaries in Iraq. Al-Qaeda was trying to push the Americans back to defending the main lines of communications and get them out of the neighborhoods. They wanted the Americans back in a defensive crouch.

MacFarland's Ready First brigade was tactically moving in the opposite direction of most U.S. forces in Iraq. The marine command in Anbar was supportive of the strategy, but the overarching plan in Iraq was for American forces to withdraw back to large bases so Iraqi forces could take the lead. The Ready First was building combat outposts and patrolling aggressively. The enemy was back in the city and fighting hard. In the first week of August the brigade had lost nine soldiers.

Some staff officers worried they would be ordered to throttle back. The spike in casualties was a direct result of tactics that were unorthodox. "Our fear was that the desire to cease operations would come from outside the brigade," Maj. Eric Remoy said. "Our concern was VIPs would come out and see what we're doing in Ramadi and the casualties we were taking and say—

without understanding what we were doing and what our end state was—and tell us to pull back on the reins.

"We would have lost momentum if that had happened."

But Marine Maj. Gen. Richard Zilmer, MacFarland's commander, believed in the plan. He knew that if he started second-guessing the colonel he might undermine his confidence at a critical time. Success was far from guaranteed, but the war would not be won unless commanders took risks. "He never picked up the phone and said, 'Goddamn it, MacFarland, what in the hell are you doing down there? You're just losing soldiers and marines,'" MacFarland said.

"I was probably questioning myself more than my boss was questioning me."

Outside of Anbar, no one gave Ramadi a lot of attention. The attention was on Baghdad, which by the summer of 2006 was near the edge of civil war.

In fact, the top command in Baghdad considered taking two battalions from Ramadi and sending them to the capital. MacFarland was alarmed when told by his higher headquarters that he might lose a couple of battalions. "They would be better off reinforcing success where they find it, like in Ramadi," he thought.

It didn't happen, but it shows how Anbar was viewed. Baghdad was the key to success—or failure. Anbar was all but written off.

"People thought he was going to fail," Gates says of MacFarland.

———

The death of Jason West, a popular staff officer, hit the staff hard. The brigade chaplain, Lt. Col. Michael Wood, knocked on MacFarland's office door shortly after he received word of the attack. "I just wanted a pulse check," Wood said.

Wood asked the colonel how he was doing? MacFarland was uncharacteristically abrupt.

"How do you *think* I'm doing?" MacFarland said.

"Sir, we're all mourning with you."

"I know," MacFarland replied. The two prayed together in MacFarland's office.

MacFarland ordered snipers out into the streets that night, planned raids for the following day, and ordered his forces to enter the Saddam Mosque, which insurgents used as a meeting place to plan attacks. A tank platoon was ordered to remain on Route Michigan until his soldiers could knock down some of the buildings favored by insurgents. That night MacFarland received word from Multi-National Corps–Iraq that his long-anticipated plans to clear Anbar University would require approval from Prime Minister Nouri al-Maliki. The brigade suspected that insurgents used it as a sanctuary to put together roadside bombs and place them on a nearby road used by American troops. But as a university it was a politically sensitive target and top U.S. commanders worried about how the Iraqi government would react to news reports about American soldiers sweeping through a largely Sunni university.

"We'll push back hard starting tonight—won't let indecision at Corps keep me from retaining the initiative," MacFarland decided.

The next morning, the brigade staff filed into the conference room in the headquarters for the daily update, taking their seats around a makeshift conference table. Most were looking down at their feet. Some looked over at the empty chair that had been occupied by Jason West.

MacFarland recounted to his staff the story of Gen. Ulysses S. Grant after the first day of the battle of Shiloh, when the Union army was mauled by the Confederates and its camp overrun. That night, Grant was under a tree in the darkness as rain poured down and his generals counseled retreat.

Brig. Gen. William T. Sherman approached Grant. "Well, Grant, we've had the devil's own day, haven't we?"

"Yes, lick 'em tomorrow though," Grant replied.

Whatever private anguish MacFarland felt from the mounting American casualties, he didn't want doubts or anxiety to blunt the brigade's offensive spirit. He turned to Grant—whose story had provided such inspiration to him as a young officer—to help him find the strength. He needed to keep the pressure on.

Five days after the attack, MacFarland told his staff he wanted to launch a pre-Ramadan offensive to ensure the enemy didn't seize the initiative during the Islamic holiday, when attacks generally go up. He wanted to build more outposts in central Ramadi and Tameem, on the western outskirts. And he wanted them completed before late October when Ramadan started.

His executive officer, Lt. Col. Pete Lee, raised concerns since there weren't enough Iraqi troops to man the outposts.

MacFarland cut him off. He wanted to keep the enemy off balance. He wanted to keep the pressure on while they still had the forces. MacFarland was still worried that some of his own battalions wouldn't be replaced when they left Iraq. There was mounting pressure in Washington to begin withdrawing U.S. troops. They had to maintain the initiative.

"We're going to do this while we have the U.S. forces available and before Ramadan," he told his staff.

MacFarland figured the enemy would only be emboldened if they let the pressure off.

"I also knew intuitively that we were inflicting a cost on the enemy too and that sooner or later that would have to be reflected in how the enemy was able to react to us," MacFarland said.

MacFarland thought again about Grant, whose career up until the Civil War was undistinguished. But in combat he had showed an almost superhuman determination and resolve. Often it was nothing more than force of will that provided the margin of victory.

At the Battle of the Wilderness, Grant's commanders began to recount what Robert E. Lee's army was capable of doing. Grant stood and said, "Oh, I am heartily tired of hearing about what Lee is going to do. Some of you always seem to think he is suddenly going to turn a double somersault and land in our rear and on both our flanks at the same time." Grant told them to start thinking about what they could do to Lee's army.

"Don't think about what the enemy is doing to you," Mac-Farland told his staff. "Think about what you can do to the enemy."

Casualties continued to mount. It was getting to the point where MacFarland worried he wouldn't make it to all the brigade's memorial services.

In late July MacFarland was at one of the almost daily hero flights. The remains of Christopher Swanson, a twenty-five-year-old staff sergeant who was killed by a sniper, were loaded into the back of a helicopter. MacFarland noticed a soldier crying hard, clinging to another man in his unit. "These young soldiers are learning in a very short time what it takes adults most of their lives to learn," he thought.

"People need to know about this place," MacFarland thought afterward. "We are attacking and the enemy is defending and counterattacking." The losses couldn't be in vain.

They needed a breakthrough. In armor terms, they needed to breach the enemy defenses.

8

Sheik Sattar

Can you persuade people to take your side when you
are not sure in the end whether you'll be there to take
theirs?

—GERTRUDE BELL, APRIL 1916

L t. Col. Tony Deane came to the U.S. Army via ROTC at
the University of Nebraska. Loud, profane, and prone to
sudden bursts of laughter, he grew up in a small windswept mid-
western town. No one expected him to make general, but he was
a plain speaker who was effective at his job as an armor officer.
He was rarely without a cigarette or cigar jutting from his mouth
except when he was working a pinch of dip. He hated meetings
and endless PowerPoint briefings. Most commanders spent a lot
of their days on the road checking on their troops. But Deane
seemed manic about being around the action. He would often
beat the quick reaction force to a firefight. "We thought he had a
death wish," says Capt. Sean Frerking, a staff officer.

In a profession that values cool analysis and brevity, Deane was emotional and could talk excitedly for hours. Some of his colleagues thought he was too combative, but most of his subordinates liked him. First Sgt. Robin Bolmer spent many late nights talking ideas and personalities with the colonel. Bolmer would smell Deane's cigar smoke drifting down the hall before he heard the familiar knock at his door. It wasn't typical for a battalion commander to bypass the company commander and go right to a noncommissioned officer to talk tactics, but that's how Deane worked. He spoke his mind to superiors, earning his combative reputation. He didn't always know when it was time to stop bitching and carry out orders.

"He wears his emotions on his sleeve," Bolmer says.

Deane would sometimes drive his staff to distraction with strange ideas. "He's not a linear thinker," Frerking said. "Sometimes he would just shoot off on a tangent."

One such tangent was an obscure sheik named Abdul Sattar Bezia al-Rishawi.

Deane's battalion arrived in Ramadi in May 2006 and was assigned to Tameem, on the city's western outskirts. The neighborhood was home to the Abu Risha tribe and Sheik Sattar's massive family compound, which was less than a mile from Camp Ramadi's front gate. Sattar had been friendly to Americans for the past couple of years. Mostly he had provided information to the U.S. military and CIA agents operating in the region. The U.S. military also occasionally contracted with Sattar's businesses. The cooperation didn't go much beyond that.

Deane figured Ramadi wasn't all that different than the place where he grew up. Only the locals could provide law and order. Foreigners would always be suspect. He assembled his staff.

"I'm going to paraphrase L.B.J." he said. "It's time for Iraqi boys to die for their country."

Killing al-Qaeda was a necessary part of the American strategy, but it wouldn't be sufficient to win. Iraqis needed to step forward if Ramadi was to be won.

Deane and Sattar would spend hours drinking sweet tea, smoking cigarettes, and talking in the sheik's compound. Deane thought Sattar could be the answer the Americans were looking for. Not that he had a lot of choice. There were few other sheiks willing to be seen with Americans.

There were few Iraqi police in the city. Many of the Iraqi soldiers were Shiites from Baghdad who were mistrusted by the Sunnis in Anbar. They were okay to conduct military operations, but they weren't designed for maintaining local law and order and providing intelligence. They needed locals to step forward and help the Americans. At the time, most people would turn away from Americans on the streets. They weren't about to join forces with them.

MacFarland and his higher command, the First Marine Expeditionary Force, understood the importance of working with tribal leaders. The civilian governor of Anbar, Governor Mamoun Sami Rashid al-Alwani, had no following. Anbar was a tribal province. Many of the tribal leaders were fighting alongside al-Qaeda against the Americans. Others were laying low or had left the country. Mamoon, a heavyset man with dark hair, was an engineer of little standing. The tribal sheiks, including Sattar, looked down on him.

From the earliest days of the Iraq War, it was U.S. policy to build a democratic, representative government in Iraq. "We started out with this Jeffersonian concept of trying to establish democracy like in the United States," says Lt. Col. Jim Lechner. Sheiks didn't fit in that picture. The thinking was that tribal sheiks were primitive throwbacks who pose a threat to representative government and modernity. Sheiks dressed in their flowing robes and head scarves would be invited to meetings, but the U.S. administration in Iraq would not give them a prominent position, fearful that they posed a threat to the civil government they were attempting to build.

It was a flawed view. The tribal system embraced elements of democracy. The sheik may not be elected, but nor is he born into his job. Sheiks are generally selected by a group of elders. "It takes consensus to create a sheik," said William "Mac" McCallister, a retired army officer who advised the marine command on tribal issues in Iraq. Some tribal leaders are wealthy and well-educated.

Throughout history, ignoring the tribes has never been a smart move. Shicks have wielded power for thousands of years and have survived countless efforts to blunt their influence in the name of modernity. The Ottomans tried to undermine powerful sheiks in Mesopotamia by taking away their land, the source of their wealth. The British returned land to them in a bid to win them over and consolidate control over the countryside. In later years, the rise of nationalism, communism, and pan-Arab ideology in Iraq always emerged accompanied with a pledge to eliminate the reactionary influence of tribes. Yet the tribes were left standing long after one ideology was replaced by another.

The key to their survival is simple: Tribes are not about ideology. They're about self-interest. That has served them well over the centuries. Ideologies come and go, particularly in Iraq, which has seen a succession of foreign rulers and a dizzying number of coups. Iraqis are used to waking up to a new government in power. The sheiks always survived.

Early on, Saddam Hussein's Baath Party made a show of opposing tribes as a drag on economic and political progress. In 1973, his government prohibited Iraqis from using tribal suffixes, like Tikriti, on their names in an effort to blunt the power of tribes. But Saddam stocked his military and intelligence posts with fellow tribesmen. And when Saddam was in trouble after the 1990-91 Gulf War, he turned to the sheiks for support, buying loyalty from selected tribal leaders with money and arms.

Previous units in Ramadi had been reluctant to jump in bed with the tribes, worrying about risk or violating American policy. "It's kind of like giving the ball to Barry Sanders," says Brig. Gen. David Reist, who was deputy commander of the First Marine Expeditionary Force in Anbar in 2006 and who worked with powerful tribal leaders who had fled to Jordan. Sanders was a National Football League running back who was all over the field. He was impossible to predict. Giving him the ball was always a leap of faith.

So was working with the tribes.

Col. John Gronski, the brigade commander in Ramadi before the Ready First arrived, said a number of sheiks had asked for weapons and permission to secure their own neighborhoods while he was in Ramadi in 2005. He said no. "The thinking at that point in time . . . was that that would not be a good strategy because we believed we had to do everything we could to legitimize the provincial government and the national government," Gronski said.

Sattar sported a well-groomed goatee and had jet black hair. He looked like Hollywood's version of an Arab sheik. In truth, most sheiks are heavyset and are used to exercising most of their power in back rooms. They don't need charisma. But Sattar was not typical. Abu Risha was a small tribe that had little influence in Anbar, where rich and powerful sheiks had held sway for centuries. Sattar's family ran a lucrative oil-smuggling business that involved getting off-the-books oil from the Bayji refinery in northern Iraq and running the contraband across the border to Syria. But they had been under the radar for years.

Sattar was rarely without his western-style Colt .44 revolver, worn under his gold-braided robes in a leather holster. He liked to drink whiskey and tell stories. He cultivated a reputation of being violent, and tales of his exploits, some involving him meting out justice personally, would follow him around. Even more eccentric was Sattar's obsession with President Bush.

"My dream in life is to meet George Bush," he would tell Deane during long, rambling talks.

"I guess you don't subscribe to *The New York Times*," Deane thought.

Perhaps only someone as iconoclastic as Deane could take Sattar seriously. "Sattar was a similar personality in that he didn't follow the rules either," Frerking said.

"Not to say Col. Deane didn't follow the rules, but he was very willing to look into other possibilities."

Sattar's charisma, and perhaps his macho reputation, helped win over American officers. He wasn't like the other sheiks, who were often overweight and rumpled. Sattar always wore a brilliant white dishdasha, or robe, and had piercing black eyes. He looked the part of the desert warrior.

One day as Deane and his operations officer, Maj. Chuck Bergman, were leaving Sattar's compound, Bergman said Sattar carried himself like an American general. He had that kind of presence.

Many of the richest and most powerful sheiks had left for Amman, Jordan, or Dubai shortly after the U.S. invasion. They were living in luxury, continuing to run their businesses and occasionally plotting their return, meeting with other exiles in the lobbies of well-appointed hotels.

Gen. David Petraeus, who would assume command of U.S. forces in 2007, regularly got e-mails from people who had run into the tribal sheiks in their salons in Amman. "Every congressional delegation that went through there, every pundit, every journalist would bump into these guys and then e-mail me and say, 'Did you know that Sheik So-and-so can solve all your problems? He can deliver the tribes.'

"Sadly, that was not reality. The fact was, they had left and the reason they had left is they were scared and they weren't going to go back until the situation was turned around."

Sattar and other mid- and low-level sheiks remained behind in Anbar. They were struggling to protect their businesses and survive. That meant cooperating with al-Qaeda. There was little cultural affinity between al-Qaeda and the sheiks, who are mainly secular Sunnis. But the sheiks had little choice. They needed protection and the U.S. military seemed unwilling or incapable of helping them.

What set Sattar apart from most other sheiks was that he was one of the few who resisted al-Qaeda from the beginning. The family was set on keeping their lucrative oil-smuggling business for themselves and al-Qaeda was muscling in on all sorts of businesses. Tribes controlled construction businesses, restaurants, and smuggling operations between Baghdad and Jordan and Syria.

"I was always against these terrorists," Sattar told a reporter. "They brainwashed people into thinking Americans were against them. They said foreigners wanted to occupy our land and destroy our mosques. They told us, 'We'll wage a jihad. We'll help you defeat them.'"

Sattar's father, Bezia Ftekhan al-Rishawi, was vocal in his opposition to al-Qaeda when fighters began filtering into Anbar after the U.S. invasion. Ftekhan confronted al-Qaeda leaders, telling them they were misinterpreting Islam in their teachings. He told them attacking innocent people and even Americans was forbidden.

After attending a funeral in 2005, Ftekhan's car was stopped. A man asked if he was Sheik Bezia Ftekhan al-Rishawi. When he said he was, the gunman shot him six times with a pistol.

Sattar and his brothers still refused to back down. They wouldn't leave Iraq. Perhaps they saw an opportunity to ultimately defeat al-Qaeda. Maybe al-Qaeda was an affront to what they believed in. Three of Sattar's brothers were killed in 2004 and 2005.

The Abu Risha tribe accumulated a blood debt against al-Qaeda. Sattar saw himself as the man who would collect.

9

Awakening

I know every tribal chief of any importance through the whole length and breadth of Iraq, and I think them the backbone of the country.

—GERTRUDE BELL

Lt. Col. Tony Deane had just returned from two weeks' leave when he and his operations officer, Maj. David Raugh, arrived at Sheik Sattar's compound one Saturday afternoon in early September for a routine visit. They were directed to the sheik's large meeting hall, next to his family residence, where he was holding court with a group of sheiks. That wasn't unusual. Sattar often had visitors. But this looked different, more formal. Some men wore suits, others sat along the walls, dressed in traditional dishdashas, or robes, with gold trim and headdresses. Sattar's meeting hall was sort of a clubhouse for sheiks. Thickly upholstered chairs and couches lined the walls. Sattar sat in the middle of the room.

The men sat around the walls. A thick haze of cigarette smoke hung over the meeting hall.

The men stopped to acknowledge Deane and his small entourage as they entered the room. Shrugging off his protective gear, Deane lit a cigar and asked Sattar what was happening.

"We're declaring independence," the sheik said.

Deane was stunned. *A tribal conspiracy?*

He was used to surprises when he came to Sattar's *diwaniya*, or meeting room. That was part of Sattar's charm. One time, Deane encountered a sheik there who was talking about raising his own private army. He was outside Deane's area of operation, so the colonel smiled and nodded while he outlined his outrageous plan.

But this was serious. Sattar handed Deane a proclamation, which contained eleven points. Deane quickly handed the document to his interpreter. It boiled down to this: The tribes were allying themselves with the coalition and declaring war on al-Qaeda. That was good. But they were also talking about establishing their own "emergency council," which meant elbowing out the U.S.-backed and -elected provincial government. The sheiks were declaring a state of emergency so they could take over the government in Anbar. Sattar was in effect appointing himself governor. This sounded like a coup.

Deane's mind was racing. The part about fighting al-Qaeda was great, but Sattar was now advocating the overthrow of the civil government that had been so carefully nurtured and protected by U.S. forces. Only a couple of weeks ago, Deane was begging Sattar to get off the fence. Now he was vaulting over it.

Deane thought fast. He said he didn't think the constitution would allow Sattar to toss out an elected government. Sattar went into another room and emerged with a couple of men dressed in western suits. They introduced themselves as lawyers. One pulled out a copy of the Iraqi constitution and started showing Deane the clause that would allow them to replace the governor if he is ineffective or corrupt.

"It was fairly legal," Deane said. "As legal as any revolution."

Deane needed time. He interrupted the lawyer's long-winded explanation.

"When do you plan on doing this?" Deane asked, turning to Sattar.

"Tuesday," he said—three days away. "Can you get CNN here?" Sattar also wanted to meet with Lt. Gen. Pete Chiarelli, the number two U.S. commander in Iraq. Evidently, Sattar had thought this through.

Deane needed time. He didn't want to discourage Sattar, but he knew he couldn't let him take over the U.S.-backed government, however ineffective it was. The United States was supposed to be for democracy. He told Sattar to hold off on CNN and Chiarelli.

"You got me on the team," Deane told Sattar.

Deane said he had to let his boss, Col. MacFarland, know about it.

Deane took a copy of the proclamation and headed for the door with his interpreter and security team in tow. He had been keeping MacFarland posted on normal meetings with sheiks in his area. But Deane wasn't sure how MacFarland would react when he told him a group of sheiks were plotting a coup about a mile from the U.S. base in Ramadi.

Deane rushed to Camp Ramadi and burst into MacFarland's office.

"Hey, sir, I've got good news and bad news," Deane told him. "Sattar is ready to get the government going."

MacFarland looked up from his desk and cocked an eyebrow.

"The bad news is he declared himself governor.

"He's looking at me like, 'What have you done now?'" Deane recalled.

This was not the first time the tribes had revolted against al-Qaeda.

In late 2005, months before Sattar's own declaration, tribal leaders had become fed up with al-Qaeda. "Generally this initial fight was over economics," said Marine Maj. Gen. Walter Gaskin, the top American commander in Anbar in 2007. "Al-Qaeda was taking it off the top and sometimes took over entire businesses." Al-Qaeda was also forcing some of their women into marriage and regularly using murder and intimidation to get their way. There was a growing rift between al-Qaeda and the sheiks, who were leading nationalist insurgent groups. The nationalists wanted Americans gone and aspired to get back into power, but they were secular and had little in common with the version of radical Islam that al-Qaeda was peddling.

Both groups were fighting the Americans, but it had always been a marriage of convenience. The insurgents had aligned themselves with al-Qaeda because they thought it was the only way to survive. The way the sheiks saw it, the Americans had kicked the Sunnis out of power, and when the U.S. military left the Sunni sheiks would be at the mercy of the Shiites. But now the sheiks realized they might be extinguished by al-Qaeda. Al-Qaeda had become a bigger threat than the Americans.

Tribal leaders formed a committee consisting of about eleven sheiks and headed by Nasser al-Fahdawi, a powerful leader of the Albu Fahad tribe, and Mohammed Mahmoud Latif, a religious leader. Fahdawi had been a physics professor at Anbar University and had been a ranking member of the ruling Baath Party. Both men were closely aligned with the 1920 Revolution Brigade, a nationalist group that was fighting the Americans alongside al-Qaeda. They had been holding talks with various Americans for months, but the negotiations had gone nowhere. The group—which they named the Anbar People's Committee—decided to oppose al-Qaeda. They stopped short, however, of allying publicly with Americans.

The environment was changing. Iraq's government had just held its second national elections in December 2005. The Sunnis had mostly boycotted the first round of elections a year earlier. This time voters in Anbar turned out in much larger numbers—about 60 percent of the province's voters, compared to about 2 percent a year earlier. In fact, there was an unwritten agreement between the Americans and local leaders, including Nasser and Latif, that Iraqis would provide for their own security during the elections. Americans would stay on their bases and local tribal leaders would ensure insurgents didn't cause any problems that would keep voters away from the polls. The marines had received a report that Nasser had captured some mid-level al-Qaeda operatives and held them in his home at gunpoint, threatening to kill them if al-Qaeda disrupted the elections. It was hard to prove, but the elections came off with little violence and Sunnis came out to vote in decent numbers for the first time.

Provincewide attack levels around that time dropped to about twenty to twenty-five a day from nearly double that. On election day children cautiously emerged from their homes to play soccer amid the rubble along Route Michigan. Maj. Ben Connable, who had just arrived for a tour as an intelligence analyst in the province, was amazed at the changes. An Arabic speaker, Connable had been to Anbar before and had as good an understanding of Anbar's insurgency as anyone in the U.S. military. It seemed to him that people in Anbar were collectively holding their breath. This, Connable thought, was an opportunity. It was a time to add troops and protect the tribes so this nascent movement could take hold. It was a chance to break the stalemate.

But the Americans didn't act to reinforce success. "Instead of that, General George Casey at the end of December came out and issued a public statement saying that the next two brigades deploying to Iraq were going to be kept back as a reserve," Connable said. "Every time we had a minor success, we would start withdrawing troops."

Al-Qaeda didn't hesitate. They would slam shut the window of opportunity before the Americans recognized it was open.

On January 5, the Americans held a massive recruiting drive for police at an abandoned glass factory on the outskirts of Ramadi. Hopes were high, coming off the successful elections and the new attitude among the tribal leaders. On the first day, two hundred local men showed up.

"We've reached a turning point here," Col. John Gronski, commander of 2-28, the National Guard brigade, told Lt. Col. Michael McLaughlin, his tribal liaison officer, as they watched men line up.

"The sheiks are really getting behind us."

On the second day, they had twice the number. The tribal leaders seemed to have given their blessing to young men who wanted to join the police. At least they were no longer blocking men from joining. "The third day we had more than five hundred standing in line," Gronski said. "We thought, 'Man, this is fantastic.'" The next day, about one thousand people showed up.

Gronski was at the factory on the fourth day. He was standing outside the factory walls that morning, admiring the long lines of recruits and thanking them individually for turning out. The Americans were ecstatic.

Gronski had an appointment with the governor and told McLaughlin he would return later that day.

"Great job," he told McLaughlin as he walked back inside the compound to get in his vehicle. "This is going really well."

He had just gotten inside the factory walls when he heard the explosion. He turned and saw smoke rising over the wall.

When he got to the scene bodies and body parts were strewn around the pavement. A suicide bomber had stood among the long line of men waiting to join the police and detonated himself. McLaughlin was lying on the ground. Soldiers were gathered around him. He didn't have a scratch on him. A single ball bearing from the suicide vest entered the back of his head under the helmet, killing him. At least fifty Iraqis died that morning and dozens more were injured.

Next, al-Qaeda turned to the sheiks who had dared to stand up to them. They put together a hit list of about a dozen sheiks. On the top of the list was Nasser. He was gunned down while getting out of his car near a market less than two weeks after the glass factory bombing. Others were decapitated or their bodies left in the streets as a warning. About nine of the eleven sheiks who were part of the original Anbar People's Committee were killed. Others fled or went to ground. Latif escaped to Syria. The bloodbath was over in two weeks. It had sent a powerful message.

Nasser's death in particular sent a chill through the province. He was powerful and had been an ally of al-Qaeda. "The message there was if Nasser could get killed any one of us could get killed," Gronski said. The tribes that were left in Ramadi were "feral" tribes. The last of the prominent leaders had left.

Al-Qaeda was surgical, thorough, and effective. "Ramadi went dark after that," said a marine intelligence officer. Violence went back up and al-Qaeda was firmly in control of the insurgency.

The slaughter occurred before the Ready First brigade arrived, but the staff had studied what happened.

"It was the night of the long knives," MacFarland said. "Al-Qaeda just cleaned house."

The Americans in Ramadi had made no effort to protect the sheiks. In fact, as the reprisals spread from Tameem in western Ramadi to the eastern parts of the city, the American forces set up checkpoints so the violence wouldn't spill over into central Ramadi.

"It sent a message of, 'You guys are on your own,'" said Maj. Eric Remoy, the intelligence officer for the Ready First brigade.

Connable was monitoring events at marine headquarters at Camp Fallujah. He was frustrated as he watched the window of opportunity slam shut.

"We had completely missed the boat on our one opportunity."

Sattar had wanted no part of the Anbar People's Committee. He had never been aligned with al-Qaeda and most of those sheiks had. He also believed it was a mistake to take on al-Qaeda without American help. For their part, the major tribal leaders didn't take Sattar seriously. He was part of a small tribe and had a reputation as a hothead and highway bandit.

"I don't trust those guys," Sattar told Gronski. "I don't like those guys."

Sattar had his own ideas.

10

"This Is Iraq"

Anybody who watched our experience in Vietnam
kind of has to really swallow hard when we say,
"Don't worry. We are not going to leave you behind."
—COL. SEAN MACFARLAND

About twenty sheiks dressed in robes and head scarves lined
the walls of Sattar's meeting hall when Deane and Mac-
Farland arrived there on September 9. Dozens of men in business suits sat alongside them. Worry beads dangled from their
hands. Sattar took MacFarland around, introducing him to the
participants. Then he sat MacFarland by his side in a large
thickly upholstered chair. MacFarland had expected to come as
an observer. He realized now that he was a key player in whatever drama was about to unfold.

Sattar began addressing the assembly, formally announcing
the formation of the Awakening. He repeated the main points
outlined in the document he gave to Deane a week earlier, hand-

ing a copy to MacFarland's interpreter with a flourish. Then he said something that stunned the American officers.

"We will consider you friendly forces if you will support us," Sattar said. "We're with whoever is against al-Qaeda."

Sattar went further. He said they would treat an attack on Americans as an attack on their own tribesmen.

Deane puffed a cigar and listened. Sterling Jensen, the American interpreter, was amazed. A sheik was publicly backing American forces. Normally, if a tribal leader cooperated it was behind closed doors. Publicly, they denounced the American presence.

A handful of the sheiks shifted uncomfortably in their seats or looked around nervously. Sattar was going out on a limb and pulling them along with him. He had little standing in the tribal hierarchy and some of the men assembled clearly wanted to hedge their bets before getting behind a man they considered little more than a highway bandit, albeit a successful one. One of the sheiks stood up to complain about American forces. Sattar cut him off. He was determined that this meeting would not play out like countless others.

MacFarland looked around the room. "There were guys who were there who had a look of determination in their eyes."

Sattar volunteered the allegiance of the men in the room. Most were second- and third-tier sheiks; men who remained behind when the prominent sheiks fled or were killed. These were the feral tribes. The last men standing.

"I want you to have the same relation you have with me with all of these people here," Sattar told MacFarland, sweeping his hand across the room.

"We have the same enemy."

Sattar said the sheiks would support the central government in Baghdad. This, too, was an important step. Anbar was a Sunni stronghold that had viewed the Shiite government with contempt. They wanted the Americans to help build ties with Baghdad.

Faisal al-Gaood, a former Anbar governor, was called on. He talked about a provision in Iraq's constitution that says if the government doesn't convene its councils then it is dissolved and an emergency government can be established. The provincial council had decamped to the safety of the Green Zone in Baghdad. The governor had no authority and couldn't survive without the protection of the U.S. Marines who guarded him twenty-four hours a day.

"Our provincial council is doing nothing for us," al-Gaood said. Al-Gaood was invited to the meeting in order to show the Americans that the sheiks weren't just launching a coup against the U.S.-backed government. This was legal. Sattar was saying the provincial governor had to go, but he wanted to show the Americans that there was legal justification for it.

Sterling Jensen, the translator who would go on to be a political adviser to the next marine command in Anbar, stood to the side and took notes in a small green cloth-covered notebook. He noted MacFarland's presence, his lanky frame almost swallowed by the ornate chair. MacFarland had a youthful face and generally spoke in a quiet voice. The sheiks weren't sure what to make of him.

It was MacFarland's turn to speak. He was desperate for Iraqi help. There was no way to win over this city without support from the Iraqis.

MacFarland said he would support the Awakening, but the the sheiks had to act within the law and support the existing government. There would be no coups. The governor couldn't be removed. "Let's modify that plank and let's talk about working within the constitution to have fair elections in the provinces," MacFarland told the sheiks. MacFarland concluded by saying they would look into the constitutional issue, but would stand by the sheiks and fight al-Qaeda alongside them.

The room erupted in applause.

Sattar grinned.

Servants swept in, carrying enormous platters with roasted lamb sitting on top of small hills of rice, and placed the food on plastic white tables at the center of the large conference room. Piles of flatbread were stacked within easy reach. The men gathered around the mounds of food and began eating. When Mac-Farland had been in Tal Afar he couldn't go to a tribal leader's home without sitting down for an enormous meal. This was the first time he had been fed at a tribal leader's home in Ramadi. It was an important sign of respect.

Until now, the tribal leaders had been moving around in the shadows, playing one side against the other. It's what tribal leaders did. It's how they survive. Only months earlier, a tentative move by tribal leaders to stand up to al-Qaeda was brutally suppressed by the militants.

Sattar had made a smart move. He knew other tribal leaders would go along so long as they could get something out of the relationship—and so long as Sattar assumed most of the risk. The other sheiks were more than willing to let Sattar be the public face on this movement. "He put himself in a position where he would take the hit," said Capt. Matt Alden, one of Deane's company commanders.

Jensen approached MacFarland as the steaming platters of food were brought in.

"What do you think?" Jensen asked him.

"I'm going to support it," MacFarland said.

That evening MacFarland recommended to his higher head-quarters, the First Marine Expeditionary Force, that they get behind Sattar's Awakening. He figured the logic was compelling. The current provincial government was all but useless. It couldn't provide security or basic services. The sheiks exercise the real power in Anbar and they will do what they want, whether the Americans like it or not. If they did succeed, the military would be in a better position if they supported it.

The next day MacFarland met with Brig. Gen. David Reist, the deputy commander of the First Marine Expeditionary Force. Reist was in charge of economics, government, and other efforts at rebuilding the province. The marines had recognized the importance of tribes going back to when Mattis and Conway arrived in Iraq in 2004. But lately they had been dealing with the more traditional "lineal" sheiks, most of whom were living in luxury in Amman, Jordan, and Dubai. The prominent sheiks were playing both sides of the fence, seeing which side would emerge the winner. Now Sattar appeared to be outmaneuvering the powerful, traditional sheiks in a high-risk gambit.

When the wealthy sheiks in Amman got wind of Sattar's move, they were dismissive. Sheik Ali Hatim was the young descendant of Ali Sulaiman, the man the British named the "sheik of sheiks" in the 1920s. He went to Amman in an effort to get some of the prominent sheiks to return to Anbar to lead their people against al-Qaeda. They refused.

The prominent tribal leaders warned Sattar and his allies against taking on al-Qaeda. It was a losing proposition and they accused the upstarts of trying to usurp their authority. "They mocked us," said Sheik Wissam Abd al-Ibrahim, an ally of Sattar's.

"You're trying to take on al-Qaeda—the ones who fought America?" Sheik Wissam was told. "They laughed at us. 'You people are simpleminded. You cannot do what you think you're going to do.'"

Some of that thinking had rubbed off on top U.S. commanders. Reist was suspicious of Sattar, a second-tier sheik with a checkered background. Reist and others had studied the tribal structure. They knew Sattar's tribe, the Abu Rishas, was historically small and had little clout in the Euphrates River valley.

Reist was also worried about undercutting support for the governor. MacFarland said he shouldn't be worried even if the governor is deposed. "We are in danger of hitching our wagon to a falling star and losing all credibility with the people," MacFarland told him. MacFarland told Reist that the marine command should take the lead in supporting the Awakening. MacFarland's brigade was responsible just for Ramadi, but the Awakening was a provincewide movement. Reist said he didn't want to be seen as supporting a coup. Marines had lost their lives protecting the governor.

MacFarland was desperate for local allies. His troops could

kill insurgents endlessly, but only an accommodation with the people would end the fighting.

The following day, MacFarland was told the C Lake area of Ramadi, an insurgent stronghold, was unusually quiet. That was odd. The CIA considered that area to hold one of the largest concentrations of al-Qaeda in Iraq. Insurgents regularly fired mortars and rockets from the area into U.S. positions. Mac-Farland thought the meeting the day prior might have something to do with the sudden change. Sattar and his allies had claimed to have killed twenty-five al-Qaeda militants lately.

After the meeting with MacFarland had ended, one of Sattar's younger brothers was excitedly talking to Capt. Pat Fagan, an officer on Deane's staff, about how he had just joined the Iraqi police. Another of Sattar's brothers was listening to the conversation and turned to Fagan, cutting off his younger brother.

"If this goes wrong, we are all dead."

Sattar was shrewd, if not as polished and educated as more prominent tribal leaders. Here was an opportunity to leap to prominence. The family had money, but an alliance with the Americans could change the tribe's place in history. Sattar was a gambler. "It was his goal to be a great man but if necessary to go down in a hail of gunfire," Capt. Matt Alden said.

MacFarland and his commanders liked Sattar personally. He fit the Hollywood image of an Arab sheik and his bravado and swagger were appealing to American military officers. They also knew he was an opportunist and the relationship would be mercenary on both sides. It took a little longer for the Americans to figure this out. Sheiks are masters at negotiating and relationships. They've been doing it for thousands of years as a matter of survival. It's in their DNA.

Americans are more open, less practiced in reading hidden motives and veiled agendas. It took MacFarland a couple of weeks before he began to understand the relationship. "I was his iron fist behind the velvet glove," he said. "He needed me as much as I needed him, if not more. It wasn't exploitive. It was symbiotic.

"Sattar figured it out before I did."

It's difficult to say what finally pushed Sattar to risk everything and throw in his lot with the Americans. His brothers and father had been killed, presumably by al-Qaeda, but Americans only had an opaque understanding of the complex intertribal rivalries in Iraq's western desert. Hatred of al-Qaeda probably played a role, as did pure opportunism.

Sattar had been watching the Americans.

From the outset, the message the Americans had been giving the Iraqis was that the U.S. military force was not an occupation army and would be leaving soon. "That was exactly what was worrying them," MacFarland said. "Al-Qaeda was saying, 'We are going to stay here forever and this is going to be the capital of our new caliphate.'

"Are you going to throw in with the Americans who are going to be gone or mind your p's and q's so al-Qaeda doesn't come and saw your head off?"

MacFarland changed the message. "Don't worry. We are not leaving."

That had to be backed up with actions.

MacFarland wanted local police. They were the key to fighting insurgencies because they were locals who lived and worked in the community.

But the glass factory bombing had created mistrust among Iraqis. "There was a perception among the general populace that we had set them up," said Maj. Teddy Gates, a policeman and marine reservist from Virginia. It wasn't true, but it had soured relations.

The Ready First began recruiting through tribes, a sort of invitation-only process that could be better controlled and protected. Gates had identified a tribe north of the Euphrates River that was willing to join the police, but they wanted a recruitment center closer to their neighborhood. Traveling through strange neighborhoods to get to a central recruiting site exposed them to attacks from al-Qaeda or rival tribes. The Americans brought them on to Camp Blue Diamond, which was nearer their neighborhood and could be protected. Recruitment skyrocketed from twenty in June to three hundred in August.

The brigade took it a step further. They built a small police substation in the Jazeera tribal neighborhood so police could serve locally. The Jazeera police station opened in July and was staffed with about three hundred police. Gates, a reservist, was enterprising when it came to supplying the tribes. Going through the U.S. system to get weapons and other supplies was a cumbersome process. Gates was part of a circle of mavericks that orbited around MacFarland.

"I was like a scavenger," Gates recalled. "I would go around and scrounge weapons, cars—anything I could get."

Gates organized a few reservists who were cops in their civilian life and set up a small workshop to rebuild the weapons, some of which were in awful shape. The police needed a light machine gun, one that produced a high rate of fire but was small enough to carry around. Al-Qaeda was heavily armed. The answer was the RPK, a Soviet-style light machine gun. "All the ones I gave them—and I gave them a ton—were all captured," Gates said.

He trained Iraqi SWAT teams using World War II–era German Mausers that they had found in enemy caches or were captured from insurgents. Gates's team taught the Iraqi police to be able to draw their weapons quickly in close quarters. "These guys were getting attacked right at home," Gates said.

This was a different partnership, a different attitude. Americans were standing shoulder to shoulder with the Iraqis.

Marine Lt. Col. Kris Stillings was attempting the same relationship with the Iraqi Army. Stillings and Deane worked out an arrangement where Iraqi officers would be able to look at classified reports before going out on operations. Often, Iraqis would provide information to the U.S. military, which then placed a secret classification on it. That meant foreigners—the Iraqis who provided the information—couldn't see the information they had supplied. "They turn in the information, someone puts a stamp on it that says 'secret, no foreign,' and they can't see it, they can't act on it," Stillings said.

"Tony made the decision that he was going to include these guys in the updates," Stillings said of Deane. It did wonders to build trust.

On June 4, an Iraqi Army checkpoint was attacked by a car bomb that killed four Iraqi soldiers, including two officers, and wounded two Americans. Stillings went to one of the regular meetings of Deane's staff. He explained to them that when Iraqi soldiers get killed their families get nothing. He asked for donations and walked off with $2,000 in cash.

He handed the stack of twenties and hundreds to a surprised Iraqi battalion executive officer and explained what the money was for.

Gates knew that al-Qaeda would attempt to attack the new Jazeera police station. It was the first police station in an al-Qaeda-dominated area. At about the same time the Ready First Brigade put a new combat outpost in the nearby C Lake area in an effort to disrupt al-Qaeda mortar and rocket fire into Camp Ramadi. Two soldiers had been killed by mortar fire as the brigade was moving into Camp Ramadi.

Al-Qaeda wasn't about to stand by while the Americans made inroads into their turf. The Americans braced for a counterattack.

They received intelligence reports that suggested al-Qaeda planned an attack for late August. In response, the brigade planned a raid on the cell suspected of plotting the attack. Before the brigade could strike, on August 21 al-Qaeda drove a dump truck filled with a flammable liquid up to the Jazeera station and detonated. The flammable liquid shot over the wall, raining flames down on Iraqi police and their American advisers. Three Iraqi police were killed and eight Americans were injured, including some who were burned horribly.

Gates was back on the U.S. base when he saw the black smoke coming from the direction of the police station. He called a cell phone of one of the American MPs that lived there. All he could hear was screaming on the other end of the phone. He hung up and raced toward the police station.

When he arrived, an American quick reaction force was already evacuating the injured. The smoking bodies of three Iraqi policemen were lying by the front gate near where the fuel truck exploded. The fuel explosion had gutted the building and destroyed the weapons inside.

MacFarland was on the scene too and asked the police chief, Col. Adnan, if he wanted to bring his police over to Camp Ramadi to recover. He refused. In fact, Adnan got tired of waiting for the Americans to put out the fires and in defiance of U.S. orders he and his men marched back into the burning compound. They raised a tattered Iraqi flag on the scorched pole in front of the station. The police, including some badly burned, began patrolling that afternoon. When it grew dark, they lit candles in the darkened compound and continued working.

The Americans were shocked. In response to previous attacks, Iraqi forces had generally backed down.

The next day Gates drove out to the police station with a truckload of captured weapons and began handing them to Adnan's police. The stores of captured vehicles also came in handy. Gates was able to get the police back on their feet quickly.

The Iraqis expected to get attacked, but in the past they felt they had been left to fend for themselves.

"They always knew bad things were going to happen," Gates

said. But the difference this time is Americans were proving to be reliable partners.

"You know, we always ask ourselves, 'Well, are they worthy allies?'" MacFarland said about the debate over whether to ally with Sunni tribes. "We need to ask that same question of ourselves and I would argue that we had not been worthy allies up until that point and, certainly, our history requires a bit of a leap of faith for anybody who wants to align with the United States."

On the same day al-Qaeda burned the Jazeera police station, the tribe's leader, Sheik Khalid Arrak, went missing. Khalid was the leader of the Ali Jassem tribe, which lived in the Jazeera area. His tribe manned the police station. He had been visiting the Obeid tribe in eastern Ramadi, attempting to convince the tribe to work with the new Americans in Ramadi. The U.S. military suspected al-Qaeda, either operating alone or through the Obeid tribe, was responsible for killing the sheik.

Sheiks had been killed before, but al-Qaeda was ramping up the terror. It was customary after such attacks to allow the tribe to retrieve the body. This time they severed the sheik's head and left his body on the streets. His head was never found. It was a horrific piece of psychological terror. In Islam it is critical to bury a body within twenty-four hours of death and the fact that the tribe couldn't locate their sheik's body panicked them.

"We have felt like men with their testicles cut off since the sheik was assassinated," a police commander told Sterling Jensen, the translator. Police patrols were dispatched to search for his body. Finally, the Ali Jassem tribe mounted an operation into the Obeid tribal area and recovered his body, about three days after he had been killed.

Col. Sean MacFarland, left, and Lt. Col. Tony Deane at Anbar University. Deane, commander of an armor battalion, developed a close relationship with Sheik Sattar in 2006. MacFarland, commander of the First Brigade, First Armored Division, gave his subordinates wide latitude. *(Photo courtesy of Sean MacFarland)*

Lt. Col. Jim Lechner, MacFarland's deputy, right, talking to Gen. George Casey, the top U.S. commander in Iraq, center, during a visit to Ramadi. Lechner could be tough and abrasive, but sheiks grew to respect him because he produced results and never made a promise he couldn't keep. *(Photo courtesy of U.S. Army)*

PFC Brett Tribble was one of the first soldiers from the brigade killed in Ramadi. His vehicle ran over an improvised explosive device during a night patrol. *(Photo courtesy of U.S. Army)*

Col. Sean MacFarland took a photo of Route Michigan near the government center shortly after arriving in Ramadi. The buildings were eventually knocked down and the rubble cleared away to deny a sanctuary to insurgents. *(Photo courtesy of Sean MacFarland)*

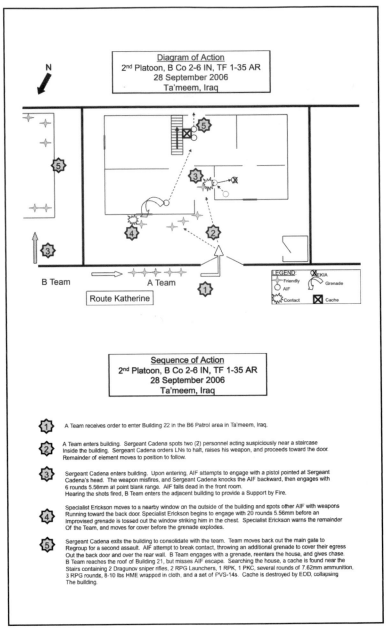

A diagram showing the firefight in September 2006 when Sgt. Jesus Cadena's team surprised a group of insurgents inside a home during a routine patrol. Cadena was awarded a Bronze Star for his actions that day. *(Diagram courtesy of U.S. Army)*

Capt. Mike Bajema, a tank commander, engaged in a series of fierce firefights when he spearheaded operations to establish combat outposts in the center of the city. *(Photo courtesy of Mike Bajema)*

Marine Maj. Gen. Richard Zilmer, left, and Col. Sean MacFarland, pose with Anbar Gov. Mamoun Sami Rashid al-Alwani, who was a John Wayne fan. The marines kept the governor alive, but he had little support among the heavily tribal population in western Iraq. *(Photo courtesy of Sean MacFarland)*

When the brigade arrived, large parts of Ramadi were abandoned and had been destroyed by intense fighting. *(Photo courtesy of Mike Bajema)*

Capt. Mike Bajema's tanks engage insurgents near Combat Outpost Grant in downtown Ramadi. *(Photo courtesy of Mike Bajema)*

A tank fires into a building on the east side of Ramadi. The Ready First brigade regularly used tanks in parts of the city that were abandoned except for insurgents. *(Photo courtesy of Sean MacFarland)*

Tanks and dismounted soldiers from 1-37 Armor patrol through Ramadi. *(Photo courtesy of Mike Bajema)*

Heavily armored Bradley Fighting Vehicles roll through Ramadi streets. *(Photo courtesy of Mike Bajema)*

Soldiers pause during a routine patrol through Ramadi. *(Photo courtesy of Mike Bajema)*

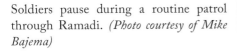

Maj. Gen. James Mattis *(left)* and Lt. Gen. James Conway *(right)*, the senior commanders in Anbar province in 2004, argued against a major offensive into Fallujah after four security contractors were killed by a mob there. They said it would play into the hands of the insurgents and derail a carefully crafted counterinsurgency plan to secure the population. Their advice was ignored by commanders in Baghdad and politicians in Washington who wanted to appear strong in the face of a challenge to American authority. That decision would mean a large number of troops were tied down in Fallujah, and Ramadi, a more important city, received fewer forces. *(Both photos courtesy of Marine Corps History Division)*

Sheik Sattar and Col. Sean MacFarland at Sattar's home. Sattar considered himself a military strategist and didn't hesitate to advise Americans on the conduct of the war. He later told President Bush he would help Americans fight insurgents in Afghanistan. *(Photo courtesy of Sean MacFarland)*

Capt. Travis Patriquin, an Arabic-speaking officer with an unconventional streak, was an early proponent of working with tribes and was outspoken in presenting his views. Patriquin was killed by a roadside bomb in December 2006. *(Photo courtesy of Gary Patriquin)*

Sheik Jassim, leader of the Albu Soda tribe, right, aligned himself with Sattar and challenged al-Qaeda. Insurgents attacked his tribe in November and the sheik turned to U.S. forces for help. The battle would prove a turning point in Ramadi's transformation. *(Photo courtesy of Marine Corps History Division)*

Col. Sean MacFarland, center, and Lt. Col. Tony Deane pose with Sattar, left of MacFarland, after MacFarland said he would support Sattar's tribal revolt against al-Qaeda. At the time of the meeting, September 9, 2006, few would have predicted the level of success it achieved. *(Photo courtesy of Tony Deane)*

Lt. Col. Chuck Ferry, commander of First Battalion, Ninth Infantry, meeting with sheiks and Iraqi military leaders to discuss operations. In November 2006, Ferry received a call from Sheik Jassim, who had come under attack in the city. Ferry's decision to lead a force to his rescue would prove critical in solidifying a tribal revolt against al-Qaeda. *(Photo courtesy of U.S. Army)*

Sheik Sattar in late 2007, shortly before his death, when his movement had grown dramatically. His home had become a salon for tribal leaders and influential government officials who gathered to talk and plot strategy. *(Photo courtesy of Matt Sanchez)*

President Bush travelled to Anbar in 2007 in order to highlight a rare success story in the Iraq war. He met with Iraqi politicians and Sheik Sattar. *(Photo courtesy of John Allen)*

Soldiers protect Air Force One during President Bush's surprise visit to Anbar in September 2007. *(Photo courtesy of John Allen)*

Sheik Ahmad al-Rishawi, the older brother of Sheik Sattar, was less charismatic, but a better administrator and less volatile than his famous brother. He assumed leadership of the Awakening after his brother's assassination. *(Photo courtesy of Marine Corps History Division)*

By 2007 Sattar had become a mythical figure and the Awakening a reconciliation movement that helped change the course of war. His death in September 2007 turned him into a martyr. *(Photo courtesy of John Allen)*

A week later, Lt. Col. Jim Lechner, MacFarland's deputy, arrived at the Jazeera police station, delivering a detainee who was the brother of the main suspect in the police station bombing. The Americans couldn't hold a suspect for long without enough evidence to convict him in an Iraqi court.

Lechner told Col. Adnan that there wasn't enough evidence to detain the suspect, but he should be told to check back in at the police station every week.

"He'll never come back!" Adnan yelled, as he flipped through the man's documentation.

"Look, let's put aside your cute ideas of democracy and human rights," Adnan told Lechner. "This is not America. This is Iraq.

"You have to rule with brutality over here."

The Jazeera police station bombing and the killing of the sheik galvanized anger that had been building for some time. Al-Qaeda had been acting with increasing brutality. They were assassinating doctors, lawyers, and engineers and anyone who they thought was cooperating with Americans or the U.S.-backed Iraqi government.

"Soon there were no men left to kill, so they started killing women and children," said the wife of a policeman in Anbar province. "They killed women and said that it was because their husbands were policemen. They killed children and said it was because their fathers were policemen."

During Ramadan in 2005 al-Qaeda hung a sixteen-year-old from a lamppost at sunset just as the imams were signaling the end of the daily fast with a prayer announced from minarets. When the last note of the prayer ended, they cut him down and let his limp body fall in the darkened street.

"They would behead a person and they would bring his head to his mother and say, 'Here's your son's head,'" said Maj. Gen. Tariq Yusif Mohammad al-Thiyabi, Anbar's provincial chief of police.

Men who were suspected of cooperating with the Americans were weighted down with rocks and thrown in the Euphrates River. When families heard gunshots they gathered their children and locked themselves in their homes. Al-Qaeda militants would then announce over loudspeakers who was about to get killed and why.

Once, when al-Qaeda militants stopped a police officer on the road and began questioning him, militants grabbed his wife by the hair and pulled her from the car. For Anbaris who had grown up with traditional tribal mores, treating a woman like that was worse than murder. Word got around.

They acted on suspicion alone when killing people. If they made a mistake they figured God would forgive them because of the righteousness of their cause, Tariq said. "They act as if they are sent from God—lawyers from God."

The tribes had had enough. Discontent was growing. They wanted to fight back, but were wary of the Americans, who until then hadn't inspired a lot of confidence. Al-Qaeda was firmly in charge. They walked around the streets without weapons, fearing nobody. "It got to the point where three or four or five people could not gather together . . . because you're exposing yourself to death if you do that," Tariq said.

Sattar and a handful of other sheiks saw something changing. "In the end the fact that they believed we would stand with them no matter what is what turned," Gates said.

Sattar noted the U.S. response to the Jazeera police station bombing. The police were getting vehicles and arms. And when they were attacked, this time the Americans were right by their side.

"He saw now by that action that we were serious about helping him, that we weren't just talking to them about fighting these guys, sending them out on their own and let them go do it while we hung back and didn't take any losses," Gates said.

"Of course, we've been taking losses all along," Gates said. But Sattar noted a change.

That al-Qaeda attacked the tribe wasn't surprising. The fact that the Americans set up a local police station and were out issuing weapons the day after the station was hit signaled something new to Sattar.

Gates was a marine and an American cop, but he knew the importance of friendship in Arab culture and was quick to pick up on local customs. He and Sattar were sitting on his couch one day holding hands, common among Arab men, when the sheik began talking about the Ali Jassem tribe.

Sattar told Gates he was interested in opening up a police station and he asked for American help.

It's exactly what Gates wanted to hear.

Sattar was also plotting behind the scenes. He spoke to his brother Ahmad about the growing anger against al-Qaeda. The two talked about contacting other sheiks and building an organization that could take on al-Qaeda.

"Leave it to me," Sattar told his older brother Ahmad. "I'll take care of it."

He called Sheik Wissam who was holed up in a village outside Anbar, asking his friend to come to his home in Ramadi to talk. Wissam was skeptical. The situation seemed hopeless. Sattar insisted. Wissam departed for Ramadi.

"We will be victorious by the God of al-Kaaba," Sattar said, as soon as he saw Wissam, dispensing with the usual lengthy greetings. Al-Kaaba is one of the holiest sites in Mecca. Sattar wasn't religious by conventional standards so the reference was unusual.

Wissam asked what he had in mind.

"I want to fight al-Qaeda," Sattar announced.

"How many men do you have?"

"Seven thousand," Sattar claimed.

Wissam knew it was a lie. Sattar might be able to muster seventy men.

11

Secret Talks

The most important thing is that we woke up from
this bad dream.

—Sheik Aifan Sadun al-Issawi

Brig. Gen. David Reist had only been in Iraq a few weeks in early 2006 when he got a brief e-mail from a Texas businessman: Get to Amman, Jordan, to attend the funeral of Talal al-Gaood.

Reist didn't bring any civilian clothes to Iraq, but there was a tailor at Camp Fallujah and he was able to cobble together a suit within hours. Reist jumped on a 2 A.M. helicopter flight to Balad, a major U.S. air base in Iraq, and from there caught a ride with a cargo plane heading to Jordan.

Talal al-Gaood was a wealthy sheik from Anbar. His funeral was a four-day affair at a magnificent government-owned convention center provided by Jordan's King Hussein. Al-Gaood, who was in his mid-forties, had died in his suite at the Ritz

Hotel in Paris where he was recovering from open heart surgery to replace a valve. He was from one of Anbar's most prominent families. He had been a key conduit for previous marine commands who were trying to get the nationalist insurgents to put down their arms and turn against al-Qaeda.

MacFarland's higher headquarters, the Marine Expeditionary Force, was working hard to convince Anbar's powerful sheiks, many of whom were living in exile in Amman and Dubai, to exercise their influence inside Iraq.

When Reist arrived in Amman he was placed in the front row of the massive hall where several hundred mourners, many dressed in gold-trimmed robes with head coverings, were paying their respects to al-Gaood. An anti-American imam was giving a fiery sermon. In attendance were mostly Sunnis, families who had prospered under Saddam Hussein's regime and were now left mainly to count their money and plot their return. To get to his seat Reist had to walk past a gauntlet of hostile glares.

At the funeral, Reist was approached by an Iraqi American businessman who asked if he would like to meet a couple of the sheiks. That evening Reist went to meet with the two men at a home in Amman. They sipped scotch and ate an elaborate meal that lasted four hours. The conversation meandered over a range of issues.

Al-Gaood had been one of the marines' main contacts and new relationships would have to be struck if the talks were to continue following his untimely death.

Reist used the funeral as a way to let the sheiks know the

marines were still interested in talking. Later, the marines followed up by holding a meeting for prominent Anbar leaders at a luxurious Red Sea resort in Jordan. The Pentagon picked up the tab for the conference and the Jordanian government provided elaborate security. On the surface, this was a business and economic conference. U.S. military leaders in Iraq didn't want to give the impression they were negotiating with Baathists, a move that would have been opposed at the top levels of the Pentagon and the State Department. Saddam's ruling Baath Party was still viewed by many in the administration as something akin to Germany's Nazi Party.

In truth, only the very top ranks of the Baath Party were filled by Saddam's henchman. The rest of the organization consisted of professionals, businessmen, and government officials who had to join the Baath Party in order to succeed. The organization had no ideology. In reaching out to prominent sheiks and former top Iraqi officers, some of whom were Baathists, the military was taking a more pragmatic approach than their superiors in Washington. The commanders wanted to get prominent Sunnis on their side in order to end the insurgency and rebuild Iraq.

Reist was approached by a CIA agent at the Red Sea resort. "Would you like to meet some people?" the agent asked. Reist and the agent went to a suite in the hotel, where two men were waiting. Reist recognized one of the sheiks he had dinner with at the funeral several weeks earlier along with another man.

"They realized they needed our help, and quite honestly we realized we needed theirs," Reist said.

The discussions led to nothing concrete, but Reist thought

reestablishing the relationships with the top-tier sheiks was critical.

The marines in Anbar were navigating through treacherous political waters. There was no mandate to reach an accord with the Sunnis. There was little direction coming from the Pentagon on the issue. Defense Secretary Donald Rumsfeld was anxious to turn the occupation of Iraq over to the State Department.

But Americans were dying in the deserts of Iraq and the American military knew that they couldn't kill their way out of the insurgency. They were left to figure it out for themselves.

The marine command had early on been slapped for attempting to set up meetings with insurgents. They would have to tread lightly so as not to raise the ire of the State Department or the high U.S. military command in Baghdad.

The Texas businessman who had e-mailed Reist was Ken Wischkaemper, a rancher and oilman with ties to Iraq and the Middle East. He lived on a sprawling ranch in the Texas Panhandle and he played a behind-the-scenes role in bringing insurgents together with the marine command.

The contacts between the marine command and the Sunni sheiks were started back in 2003 after a chance meeting between Wischkaemper and Talal al-Gaood. Wischkaemper had sold forage seed to Iraq's government before the UN imposed sanctions in 1990. After the U.S.-led invasion he was asked by a U.S. contractor to come to Iraq because of an outbreak of hoof-and-mouth disease among cattle in western Iraq. Records indicated that Saddam's regime had bought a vaccine, but the U.S. administration couldn't find it and the United Nations had left Baghdad after their headquarters was bombed. Wischkaemper's job was to track down the vaccine.

It didn't take long. "The vaccine was sitting at the airport," Wischkaemper said. "Nobody knew it was there, except the Iraqis." It was typical of how the United States' massive military operation in Iraq was foundering, Wischkaemper figured.

On his way to Iraq, the Texas businessman met al-Gaood in the elegant lobby of the Amman Four Seasons, a rendezvous spot for wealthy Iraqi exiles and other rich Gulf Arabs. The meeting was arranged by a company they had both worked for. They agreed to meet again.

On the way home in December 2003, Wischkaemper had dinner at al-Gaood's large home in Amman. Al-Gaood poured out his frustrations, hoping Wischkaemper would bring his message to influential Americans. They sat in al-Gaood's massive dining room, eating an elaborate meal and speaking for three hours.

"We are marginalized," al-Gaood told Wischkaemper. Prominent Sunnis were shoved aside, al-Gaood said.

"We have no voice in Washington. We can't talk to anyone. It's not the way it should be."

Al-Gaood seemed desperate. He had no other way to contact Americans. Wischkaemper was sympathetic. He thought the Americans had botched the war by turning their backs on the Sunnis who had run Iraq for decades.

The next day Wischkaemper flew home. On the flight he

thought a lot about the dinner with al-Gaood. Wischkaemper had no government or military experience, but he figured he could help.

He decided to return to Amman in March 2004 on his own tab to gauge how serious al-Gaood was. "I had to see if these people were for real."

The Texas businessman spent several days with al-Gaood at his business, which was headquartered in a gleaming six-story building in downtown Amman. A parade of powerful Sunnis, many former members of Saddam's regime, passed through the office while Wischkaemper was there. Wischkaemper said he felt as if he was in the presence of a "shadow government" at al-Gaood's office. He was convinced al-Gaood was who he said he was—and more.

The al-Gaood family had close ties to Saddam Hussein's government and had amassed staggering wealth over the years. They had played a role in helping Saddam's regime smuggle oil to avoid sanctions before the U.S.-led invasion by setting up a network of front companies. Then, in 1996, Talal al-Gaood ran afoul of the government and was arrested by the regime for "unspecified financial and contractual problems related to deals" with Saddam's Agriculture Ministry.

Back in Washington Wischkaemper started working contacts in an effort to reach the right people in the military. He ended up in the Pentagon office of Jerry Jones, who was serving as a special assistant to Rumsfeld. A Texan with a courtly manner, Jones was an experienced Washington hand who had started his career in the White House under Nixon and Ford.

Jones had traveled to Iraq in January 2004 as leader of an assessment team to recommend how best to transfer authority from the Coalition Provisional Authority to the State Department. One of his conclusions was that U.S. administrator Paul Bremer had failed to reach out to Iraq's key constituencies, including powerful Sunnis.

Jones was impressed by some of al-Gaood's ideas, as conveyed by Wischkaemper. Al-Gaood had proposed a constitutional convention as a way of creating a new, more representative government. Sunni leaders were mistrustful of Shiites and some of the exiled politicians backed by the United States.

Jones, who knew his way around Washington bureaucracies, concluded a constitutional convention wouldn't fly, since it would conflict with Bremer's role of establishing Iraq's new government.

"What we need to do is transform that idea into an economic conference on how to get the economy in Iraq started again," Jones said.

"By the way, while you were doing that we probably ought to address all these governance ideas that you have."

The three-day conference took place in July 2004 at the Sheraton in Amman. It was organized and funded by al-Gaood and was packed with powerful Sunnis, but also representatives of Kurds and Shiites. There were more than a hundred participants who were organized into subcommittees centered on security, governance, economics, and tribal issues. Simultaneous translations were available through headsets. Most of the speeches were critical of U.S. policy.

The small American delegation, which included Jones, a few Marine Corps officers, and others, were astounded at the level of organization, sophistication, and power in the conference. Here were influential and capable Iraqis who might be able to help end the violence. And the U.S. government hadn't reached out to them yet.

They had plenty of complaints about the U.S. military, but the Americans also saw common ground.

"All of a sudden I realized these guys are seriously organized," says Marine Col. Mike Walker, a civil affairs officer who flew in from Anbar for the meeting.

"This is the insurgency. This is the political piece of the insurgency."

Walker was an advocate of the talks. He was frustrated that the marines' counterinsurgency plan in Anbar had been derailed when they were ordered to attack Fallujah against their recommendations. That decision handed the initiative to the insurgents, Walker concluded. "We threw our campaign plan away."

Walker was convinced that the negotiations could help reduce violence.

Halfway through the first day, al-Gaood approached Jones. A "messenger" from the insurgents wanted to meet the Americans, al-Gaood told Jones.

Jones, Walker, and a handful of other Americans arranged to meet the man in the late afternoon in Jones's suite at the Sheraton. They were waiting there when a rather nervous man dressed in khakis and a blue jacket knocked on the door. The Americans settled into chairs in the plush hotel suite, which had a fireplace and a balcony with commanding views of Jordan's sprawling capital. They began talking. The messenger remained nervous and seemed worried that someone might throw a bag over his head and take him prisoner. "He was afraid for his safety," said Marine Lt. Col. Dave Harlan, who was at the meeting and took notes.

The insurgent identified himself as Dr. Ishmael and said he had been trained as a physician and an attorney. Ishmael claimed to represent sixteen insurgent groups and spoke rapidly. He refused to drink the water or juice that was served.

The messenger launched into a familiar litany of complaints. He talked about the treatment of prisoners at Abu Ghraib and said the U.S. and interim Iraqi government lacked credibility. The messenger wanted U.S. forces to pull out of major cities.

He said he had no objections to U.S. companies helping to rebuild Iraq and agreed that security was needed before the economy could grow. The messenger then asked that the Americans keep the meeting secret. The meeting broke up with an agreement to keep the line of communication open and that al-Gaood would act as a conduit for further contacts.

When higher-ups in the chain of command got wind of the meeting they were not pleased. Army Gen. George Casey, then top U.S. commander in Iraq, called the Amman rendezvous and a related economics conference a "goat rope," military slang for a chaotic mess, and said the marine headquarters lacked the authority to hold such meetings outside Iraq.

Casey appeared troubled by the military playing a diplomatic role and felt they had not coordinated properly with the State Department. In an e-mail message he said the marine headquarters "has no authority in Jordan and should plan no action there."

Marine Gen. James Conway, the top U.S. commander in western Iraq in 2004, wanted to press ahead with whatever avenue would help them achieve a political reconciliation, including talks with tribal and insurgent leaders. America's beef was with al-Qaeda, not with every former Baathist in Iraq.

"Our objectives remain to reduce attacks and get at the essence of the insurgency in Anbar," Conway wrote in an August 30, 2004, e-mail reply to Casey and the number two U.S. commander, Lt. Gen. Thomas Metz. "I consider the discussions a non-kinetic approach to a military objective and believe we should pursue that option, whether it occurs in Ramadi, al Qaim or Amman."

"What Gen. Conway was trying to do was keep this line alive until we could convince the entire chain of command that it was worth pursuing," Walker said.

The odds of that happening were not good.

In Washington, officials were no happier than Casey. Paul Wolfowitz, Rumsfeld's deputy secretary and architect of the Iraq War, didn't like that the Americans were meeting with former members of Saddam's regime, whom he had likened to Nazis. He ordered Jones to "cease and desist."

Walker, who was enthusiastic about the overtures, helped set up a test to determine if the messenger and the men he represented could deliver. The insurgents would mandate a three-day cease-fire during which they would stop attacks on Iraqi and coalition forces.

"If they're in charge of the insurgency then they should be able to prove it," Walker figured.

They agreed to meet in Iraq to work out the details. Shortly after Walker returned to Iraq a marine intelligence officer in Fallujah reported that an insurgent was asking for Walker by name.

The two met in a safe house outside Fallujah and Walker laid out the cease-fire request. The "senior leadership of the Marines requires the resistance to halt all attacks on Marines in al-Anbar and northern Babil provinces beginning at midnight on 25 July and ending on midnight 28 July," according to Walker's notes from the meeting.

Meanwhile, tensions between the State Department and the marines continued to grow. Harlan, who was serving as a marine liaison in the U.S. embassy in Amman, was ordered to leave by the military attaché in the U.S. embassy. "I was given a couple weeks to clear out," Harlan says. A marine liaison was allowed back in the embassy about a year later.

Conway's chief of staff in Iraq, Col. John Coleman, was denied permission to come through Jordan on his way back from a trip to the United States in August 2004, Harlan said. Coleman, a blunt-talking marine officer with a stellar career, was already in the air when the order was issued and was allowed to remain in an Amman hotel before continuing on to Iraq.

The April 2004 Fallujah battle and the lack of support from the top State Department and Pentagon officials would all but kill the communications between the Americans and insurgents. "Everyone got focused on the fight, the fight didn't turn out like they [the insurgents] planned, and that whole line of communication went dormant for the rest of 2004 and 2005," Walker says.

Dormant, but not dead. In late 2005, al-Gaood called Wischkaemper at his ranch in Texas with a request. Al-Gaood had just received a call from a tribal leader in western Iraq near the Syrian border. The sheik's tribe, Albu Muhal, was under attack by al-Qaeda and was in danger of being wiped out. Could the marines help?

Wischkaemper called Jones and the two of them reached Coleman, who had finished his tour in Iraq and was now base commander at Camp Pendleton.

Within hours of al-Gaood's plea, Marine Corps Cobra helicopter gunships were racing over the desert toward al-Qaim. The air strikes helped break the al-Qaeda attack and win over the Albu Muhal tribe to the U.S. side.

It was a payoff for those early efforts to talk with insurgents, according to the Americans involved.

"These guys trusted us enough to ask us to come help and we did," Jones says.

Al-Qaim was one of the rare times the prominent sheiks in Amman were able to deliver. The town was an isolated outpost on Iraq's border. The tribal cooperation didn't spread.

The cease-fire that Walker had negotiated failed. The marines saw no noticeable reduction in violence during the July 25–28 time period. It was a major disappointment. Walker thought the cease-fire didn't work because the two sides hadn't established enough trust and negotiated long enough. He wasn't ready to give up. But the failure was probably a sign that the rich exiled sheiks couldn't deliver. They had lost their influence, what the Arabs call *wasta,* when they fled Iraq. Anbar's young men had succumbed to al-Qaeda appeals and propaganda and their parents were at the mercy of al-Qaeda's murder and intimidation. The prominent sheiks weren't there to protect them.

Now it was Sattar's turn.

12

Angel on the Shoulder

The shaikh's usefulness to the English may initially
have been a mere expedient.

—HANNA BATATU

Sattar reclined in front of the television in his living room.
Sitting at a table on the other side of the room, Capt. Matt
Alden and an intelligence officer were speaking to an Iraqi and
scribbling furiously in their notebooks. The man appeared nervous, but he answered questions from the Americans, who sipped
sodas and ate food laid out by Sattar's staff. The Iraqi was providing pure gold: intelligence on the whereabouts of wanted al-
Qaeda cell leaders. Sattar had ordered the man to appear at his
home to meet with the Americans and tell them what he knew.
The man didn't appear happy about his assignment, but he was
cooperating.

Since Sattar had agreed to work with the Americans, intelligence was pouring in. It seemed Sattar and his tribal allies knew everything there was to know about the insurgency. If he didn't have personal knowledge he could find someone who did. Alden's unit, Charlie Company of Task Force 1-35, went out almost every night on raids during the summer and fall. The Americans were no longer foundering around, doing massive sweeps that yielded little but angered locals. Now the raids were targeted and they were grabbing hard-core al-Qaeda. Alden's company captured more than a hundred people in the Zangora area of Ramadi in a few months.

A U.S. officer would regularly visit the CIA station in Ramadi to get a list of wanted al-Qaeda operatives. The Americans would then discuss the list with Sattar. He knew everybody.

Sometimes Sattar would protect people. "This guy is on your list but don't go after him," Sattar would often say.

"He's close to me. He's told me everything. I can control him." The Americans would generally defer to Sattar. His status was growing.

A retired commander in Fedayeen Saddam, a paramilitary organization loyal to the Baath Party, brought a list of fifty al-Qaeda-linked insurgents to the Americans. He also offered the services of twenty-five men who were loyal to him and could lead the Americans to the targets.

Sattar was convincing other tribes to flock to his banner. The sheiks got benefits from allying themselves with the Americans. They would get a police station, complete with weapons and vehicles. More important, the tribe's young men would get paying jobs. Many had previously been planting roadside bombs for money. As tribes flipped, attacks against Americans in their areas generally ceased. They were able to stand up to al-Qaeda and protect their turf.

The sheiks who had remained in Ramadi were growing in power. They were providing for their people. Better yet, Sattar was assuming much of the risk and providing cover for other sheiks who came over to the Awakening. He was the public face of the growing movement.

The sheiks were also free to conduct their own small operations. There were blood debts that couldn't wait.

American forces were finding bodies scattered on the streets of Ramadi. Some were al-Qaeda leaders who had been wanted by the U.S. military. On September 16, a week after the meeting to form the Awakening, MacFarland received a number of intelligence reports about a group of men entering a mosque. The gunmen asked the worshipers to identify al-Qaeda members in their midst. They pointed them out. About ten men were marched outside and shot.

Soon the Americans were hearing reports of a shadowy organization called Thuwar al-Anbar. The Americans saw it as the military wing of the Sawah al-Anbar, or the Awakening. One of Sattar's bodyguards described it to Capt. Travis Patriquin as a group of friends or relatives who share a blood debt against al-Qaeda. The debt was usually incurred because a relative was killed, a car stolen, or a family was forced from their home. Sometimes the debt was incurred because a sister was forced into marriage with an al-Qaeda fighter. Payback was usually death.

Sattar and his entourage opened up to Patriquin. He spoke Arabic, cultivated a bushy black mustache to blend in with Iraqis, and developed a deep bond with Sattar and some of the other sheiks. He became a fervent supporter of the strategy to work with tribes and was impatient with anyone who failed to see that tribes were the key to what passed for victory in Iraq. Sattar gave Patriquin an Arabic name, "Wisam," or warrior, and would greet him with the traditional embrace and kiss when they met. Patriquin would often accompany Lechner or other officers over to Sattar's home. While Lechner talked business with Sattar, Patriquin would often pull aside a minor sheik or distant cousin and glean valuable information. The Iraqis loved Patriquin. He probably knew the tribes in Anbar better than any American there.

MacFarland asked Patriquin to prepare a brief for the First Marine Expeditionary Force staff, many of who remained skeptical of Sattar and his tribal allies. MacFarland wanted Patriquin to explain that he wasn't a "Colonel Kurtz" who had gone off the reservation and was arming tribes. Patriquin came up with a PowerPoint presentation.

"This is a sheik," the PowerPoint slide says below a stick figure with a kaffiyeh on his head. "They've been leading the people of this area for approximately 14,000 years." It was written in an irreverent style, but it revealed Patriquin's understanding of Iraqi tribes. The PowerPoint went viral on the Internet and is still used by some army officers to teach the concept of working with tribes.

Patriquin developed a friendship with one of Sattar's nephews, a twenty-five-year-old who was part of the sheik's security detail. After lunch one day, he pulled the man aside to talk about Thuwar al-Anbar, the Awakening's armed wing.

"TAA doesn't exist as an organized force," the bodyguard told Patriquin.

"What TAA is, is a group of friends or relations who have been wronged by al-Qaeda in Iraq in the past and want revenge."

Patriquin told him that a "group of Americans" were interested in assisting the organization.

They weren't interested in help from the Americans, the man replied.

Patriquin told him that by helping establish Iraqi police the United States was indirectly supporting Thuwar al-Anbar since many of the men are off-duty police.

The bodyguard grinned broadly.

Some of the vigilante action started before the Awakening, but the activity increased after its formation. The group used terror tactics against al-Qaeda: attacking at night, wearing masks, and using the Opels favored by the militants. They would sometimes leave bodies in the streets with signs around their necks, identifying them as al-Qaeda to strike fear into colleagues who were still at large.

Americans urged the Iraqis to coordinate more with U.S. forces. At night, it was getting hard for the Americans to tell the tribal vigilantes from al-Qaeda. On several occasions, the Americans mistakenly got in firefights with Sattar's people. Once American soldiers killed a man creeping through the streets with a ski mask over his face. It turned out it was one of Sattar's people on his way to assassinate an al-Qaeda operative in central Ramadi.

"Sometimes they'd screw up and do it in daylight and all we'd see is a guy in a ski mask and a gun and we'd shoot him," Lechner explained.

The Americans and their Iraqi allies would work out secret signals so as not to accidently kill tribesmen. "They would put their AK-47 on the ground and lift up their arms and the snipers would know, okay, these guys are going to do their thing," Jensen said. "They would let them go do it."

The Americans figured most of the victims were people they wanted killed or captured anyway. They were careful about not officially sanctioning any of these actions. "We could not condone, associate with, or support the existence of TAA because they were working outside the rule of law," said Maj. Eric Remoy, the brigade's intelligence officer.

But unlike previous units, the Ready First did not see this as "red-on-red" violence. These attacks were working to the Americans' advantage. They would make no effort to stop them.

On October 25, 2006, al-Qaeda militants beheaded three teenagers in the Sofia district of Ramadi. Sattar's Awakening retaliated. They grabbed an al-Qaeda militant and publicly executed him in Ramadi's streets.

The Sunnis in Anbar saw a distinction between the "honorable" resistance, secular Iraqis resisting the American opposition, and al-Qaeda, religious extremists who wanted to establish an Islamic caliphate, or rule, over the Arab world. The "honorable" resistance were former Baathists and others who had lived well under Saddam's rule. They were educated and lived comfortable lives. They had everything to lose by the U.S.-led invasion and little to gain.

Sunnis had been running things in Iraq for centuries. The Ottomans backed a mostly Sunni officer corps in Iraq when they controlled it and the British established a Sunni monarchy after World War I. America's enthusiasm to destroy the Baath Party was read by Sunnis as a message that they had little future in Iraq. Their fears were reinforced by the U.S. decision in 2003 to disband the Iraqi Army, an institution of enormous importance to Sunnis.

If Sattar was taking a chance by joining with the Americans, MacFarland was also rolling the dice. Many of the new police recruits the tribes were bringing in had fought and killed Americans. Now their fates would be tied together.

What was really turning the tide in Ramadi was not the shadowy vigilantes darting around the Ramadi streets at night. It was an extremely visible effort to support Sattar by employing the men in his tribe as police. The Ready First brigade changed recruiting tactics. No longer would the Americans hold a massive recruiting drive open to anybody. The glass factory bombing in January showed such operations were hard to secure. Instead, the Ready First would work with specific tribes. That ensured "operational security." The tribes would want to keep it quiet to protect their own people.

Sattar agreed to hold a recruiting drive inside his own compound on July 4. The U.S. provided security, positioning tanks and Humvees around the compound. Dozens of men showed up to join the police. The Americans were amazed by the turnout. It didn't take long for al-Qaeda to figure out what was going on. They lobbed about six mortars inside his family compound while the recruiting was taking place. It damaged a few vehicles, but no one was hurt. Sattar was nonplussed. The recruiting continued.

"I'm going to have some more for you guys next week," Sattar casually told Deane. "We can do it again here."

Deane was surprised. This was Sattar's own house, his wife, his kids were there. "You are on the team at that point."

Other sheiks were watching Sattar and soon they too wanted police stations. Convincing Sunnis in Anbar to join Iraq's fledgling army was difficult. Joining the army meant you might be deployed elsewhere in Iraq. The money was attractive, but no one wanted to take the chance of leaving their family to fend for themselves when violence was raging in their city. The Ready First was willing to place police stations in tribal areas so they wouldn't get shipped to another part of the province or country.

The brigade, however, was running into Iraqi and U.S. bureaucracy in establishing the police stations. Iraq's government had regulations that dictated how many police stations could be established in a city. The U.S. military was bound to follow those rules. There was no room in the regulations for small stations in tribal areas along the lines that the Ready First wanted to establish.

The brigade decided to call them substations. The regulations didn't apply and they could build all they needed.

MacFarland chose Lt. Col. Jim Lechner as his point man on tribal and police issues. Lechner was a Citadel graduate and former Army Ranger who was shot on the streets of Mogadishu and almost lost his leg. His harrowing ordeal on the streets of the Somali capital was detailed in *Black Hawk Down*.

"Try to find out who our friends are," Lechner told his staff shortly after arriving in Ramadi.

Lechner was an unusual choice for tribal liaison. His type A personality was often at odds with the indirect approach preferred by the Arabs. When Lechner visited Ramadi's hospital and found it covered with al-Qaeda propaganda he confronted the Iraqi security guard there. One of the signs ordered the hospital staff to abide by the "Mujahideen Factions of Anbar."

"Tell your friends who put up these signs that I would like to see them," Lechner told the security guard.

"We won't speak Arabic or English. We will speak the language of guns."

He walked off, leaving the Iraqi security guard stunned.

Jensen, who translated for Lechner, sometimes grew frustrated at Lechner's abrupt approach to the Iraqis. Often Lechner would mutter about the Iraqis' whining when they would ask the Americans about providing electricity to a police station.

"I don't think Jim was beloved by the tribes," MacFarland said. He could be exhausting in his demands for police recruits. "He used to hit them over the head. 'You said four hundred guys, you had three hundred and ninety-nine there. Where was the four hundredth guy?'"

Lechner understood the need to build local police. And

slowly, the Iraqis came to respect him. He was abrupt, but he wouldn't make a promise that he couldn't deliver on. They came to depend on him.

"He who delivers the quickest, gains respect the quickest," Jensen wrote one night in his journal.

The Ready First was delivering.

Iraq's Interior Ministry was responsible for arming the police, but the U.S. officers always made sure they had plenty of captured weapons on hand to tide them over until the bureaucracy got moving. The machine guns that Gates provided the cops with ensured they could match al-Qaeda's firepower even if it wasn't part of the issued weapons.

Making sure the Iraqi government paid the Iraqi police was a constant headache. When the Americans needed extra danger pay to encourage some of the police from outlying areas to come to Ramadi's downtown, which remained deadly, Ready First officers convinced the CIA to come up with the extra money. The agency had a lot more discretion and fewer strings attached to the cash they could spread around.

The brigade was given a lot of latitude from its higher headquarters. Apologizing later was easier than asking permission first.

The confidence of the locals was building. Al-Qaeda was no longer the ten-foot-tall enemy. Al-Qaeda was fighting back hard, but now Iraqi police were holding their ground. By mid-September MacFarland noted that the Iraqi police were showing more resolve and were being intimidated less. Al-Qaeda was now focusing on attacking Iraqi police, a sure sign that their strategy was working.

A police station would get attacked by a car bomb and repairs would begin the following day.

At his house one day, Sattar patted his shoulder and told him American forces now sit there just as an angel sits on the right shoulder of all good Muslims.

13

Sympathy for the Devil

I'll freely say it now: I was wrong [about Sheik Sattar]. We should have just jumped in with both feet.
—MARINE COL. PETE DEVLIN

Sattar had spread a large piece of paper on the ground and leaned over it, mapping out his plans for securing Ramadi.

"First, burn or capture all the boats between Tameem and Ramadi and the Albu Faraj area and northern Ramadi," he instructed. No one fishes anymore in the Euphrates around Ramadi anyway. The boats are used only to transport munitions and fighters, Sattar said, warming to his plans.

"This would channelize the enemy into using our checkpoints and make him easier to capture."

Perhaps noting a skeptical look from Capt. Travis Patriquin, Sattar added a chivalrous note: If anyone could prove he was a poor fisherman, Sattar would personally purchase food for that man's family for the duration of the operation to clean the city.

It was vintage Sattar. Bold, decisive, and outlandish.

MacFarland's higher headquarters remained worried about the brigade's alliance with Sattar. The marine headquarters had a number of legitimate concerns about Sattar. First, he was a minor sheik and any relationship with him could undermine efforts to get the powerful sheiks back to Anbar from their exile in Amman, Jordan. Second, U.S. policy was to back the civil government in Iraq and Sattar and his tribal allies didn't disguise their hatred of Anbar's governor and provincial council. Sattar initially proposed what amounted to a local coup. And third, Sattar's background raised red flags. Smuggling was a way of life, but there were reports of his killing people that raised concerns.

"When I look at him I look into the eyes of a shark," one marine officer said. "He's an egomaniac."

The relationship with Sattar was causing tension between the brigade and its higher headquarters.

In the fall, Sattar's SUV barreled through a border checkpoint that was manned by U.S. and newly trained Iraqi border police. The Iraqis, and possibly the Americans, opened fire on the vehicle as it sped past.

The staff officers at Camp Fallujah were furious.

"Your guy just barreled through," MacFarland was told.

"Yeah, he's probably smuggling something," MacFarland acknowledged.

Here was another example of Sattar flaunting the rules. They wanted to arrest him when he came back across the border into Iraq. MacFarland argued that his work bringing security to Ramadi outweighed whatever smuggling operation he was involved in.

"Whatever he's smuggling is not as important as what he's doing here," MacFarland said. "So when he comes back through, let him in. I'm not going to arrest him over that.

"We talked about it and eventually we all came to the conclusion that it just wasn't worth it," MacFarland said.

Lt. Col. Tony Deane and Marine Brig. Gen. David Reist were walking through a newly built police station on the outskirts of Ramadi when the discussion turned to Sattar and the Americans' growing relationship with him.

"The guy's a criminal," Reist told Deane. "We shouldn't be dealing with him."

To drive his point home Reist said Sattar should be arrested. Reist was the deputy commander of the First Marine Expeditionary Force, the Ready First brigade's higher headquarters. He was heavily invested in ongoing talks with the traditional sheiks in self-imposed exile in Amman, Jordan.

Deane was one of MacFarland's battalion commanders and a key conduit to Sattar, whose family compound was in Deane's area of operations.

"I'm not arresting him," Deane shot back.

Deane was skeptical of the traditional cultural training the U.S. Army gives its troops. They focus on rules like not showing the soles of feet, eating with the right hand, and learning phrases. All were useful, but missed the larger point. The problem, as Deane saw it, is that Americans didn't understand generational hatreds. As a first-generation Irish American, Deane thought he had a better sense of that than most. He also figured the

Godfather movies provided a better cultural insight into the tribes than most academic books.

"You think the end of the world is showing people the bottom of your shoes?" Deane said. "They're getting their families killed. They could give a shit about that."

Deane was gregarious and talkative. He and Sattar had grown genuinely close, spending hours drinking tea and smoking cigarettes at Sattar's compound. Deane was over at Sattar's house three or four times a week.

One day a couple of weeks before Sattar formed the Awakening, Deane came over to Sattar's house and found him and a handful of sheiks sitting around talking. At the time the Americans were trying desperately to convince the tribes to join the police. Deane made his usual pitch. "There was some hemming and hawing," he said.

"You all look the same to me," Deane finally blurted out. His translator looked ashen. He said he couldn't tell the sheiks that. It was an insult.

Deane insisted. The translator spoke and the sheiks shifted in their seats.

"Listen, if you were in Nebraska we'd all have cowboy hats and plaid shirts and belt buckles, blue jeans, and cowboy boots." They had watched westerns so they could visualize what he was talking about.

"You couldn't tell who the hell was who. If you go back to Nebraska I can look everybody in my hometown in the eye and I can tell you who the good guys are, whose brother is a knucklehead, whose father was a knucklehead."

Deane said only they would be able to help the Americans

separate the good from the bad in Ramadi. The sheiks nodded in agreement.

The marine headquarters went to work putting together a file, trying to figure out who this guy was. "He wasn't anyone of any notoriety in particular so we had to kind of dig into him," said Col. Pete Devlin, the top intelligence officer in Anbar. "Sure enough there was enough information found on him that we had on file."

None of it was good. Sattar was responsible for a large smuggling operation that brought oil from the Bayji refinery to the Syrian border using forged papers. The operation would sell the oil to the Syrians at a discount. They were making a fortune. It got worse. A secret message based on reporting from the MEF's Economic and Political Intelligence Cell said Sattar was linked to the November 2005 killing of an Iraqi border official at Walid, a town on Iraq's Syrian border. The e-mail said he regularly bribed or threatened border officials and also had links to people associated with al-Qaeda.

"He is an absolutely massive crook," the secret e-mail said.

As late as March 2007, Americans remained wary of Sattar and struggled to understand how the tribes worked. "Money and political power could be his undoing," a classified intelligence report concluded. "Sattar has a history of immoral behavior where money is concerned."

There was little doubt Sattar ran a large smuggling operation in the western desert. The allegations of murder and intimidation are sketchier. Informants are often unreliable and their motives are obscure. The U.S. military couldn't run down every allegation.

"There was talk that he had personally killed people and that he had his own jail in his compound," Devlin said. "None of that could be proven. He wasn't dumb enough to let himself be caught doing that."

Sattar, thirty-five, had been arrested a couple of times in the chaos of the early war years, but had been released after short detentions. He had also cooperated with the U.S. military and the CIA, who had regarded him as a useful, if somewhat eccentric, contact. Rival businessmen accused Sattar of using his American contacts to win lucrative contracts and then strong-arm rivals.

American interrogators who encountered him were puzzled. He had said he only completed high school, but interrogators noted his evident intelligence. He said he didn't regularly attend mosque. He was drafted into the Iraqi Army, but deserted shortly afterward in 1991, around the time of the Gulf War. He was caught and served six months in jail. Interrogators concluded his main business was smuggling.

Sattar himself cultivated an image of intrigue and hinted at violence when it served his ends. There was the large revolver strapped to his hip and his talk was testosterone-fueled. He understood the importance of image. He had his own media plan and was always available to Arab satellite television, which Iraqis followed religiously. He worked it well. Al-Jazeera's English-language service caught up with him at his hotel suite in Amman, Jordan, on his way back to Iraq at one point as he was emerging as a key figure.

"To the terrorists I say that I will be in Anbar in five days," he said, staring into the camera.

"If they want to see me I'm ready for them," he said.

"It's mythmaking pure and simple," says William McCallister, a retired army officer who served as a special adviser to the marines in Iraq on tribal issues.

Deane found Sattar's rhetoric endearing. It wasn't how most sheiks talked. "It had a World Wrestling Federation feel to it," Deane said. "'On Saturday, there will be a smackdown of al-Qaeda. The streets will run red with the blood of the terrorists. . . .'

"You couldn't help but love him for it. It inspired confidence in those around him."

Sattar videotaped every meeting and made sure local reporters were notified when he wanted to speak. The public ate it up. This wasn't the Americans speaking ill of al-Qaeda. This was one of their own. Sattar wasn't playing both sides of the force.

Americans speak in measured tones, careful to avoid hyperbole. Iraqis wanted to hear their leaders speak with bravado, talking about blood running in their streets. Saddam and other Iraqi leaders had done it for years.

Sattar and his allies boasted of their successes, often exaggerating. "Even if only 2 percent was true and 98 percent was false, well, when the terrorist heard it, it's grand, it's big," said Sheik Abdul Rahman al-Janabi. The sheiks started a rumor that one sheik put captured insurgents through a mechanical grinder.

The American military struggled to separate Sattar from the myth he created.

There was a persistent tale of Sattar gunning down a rival at a Ramadi gas station. Deane heard the story from an intelligence officer attached to the Navy SEALs. According to this version, a couple of men were following Sattar in September 2006. He pulled into a gas station, got out of his car, shot and killed one of the men and injured the other.

"Sattar, did you shoot some guys?" Deane asked Sattar when he next saw him.

He smiled.

That's why the marine headquarters was worried.

"God only knows what this guy is going to do in Ramadi," Devlin said. "Turn it into his own personal fiefdom?"

Sattar and some of the other sheiks would regularly ask to be given control over their area so they could mount their own military operations. Sattar even asked to borrow American tanks.

"We're not going to give you your own AO," MacFarland said, referring to area of operations. "Give us the intelligence and we'll take care of these guys."

MacFarland understood the worries of his higher headquarters, but Sattar was worth the rush, he argued.

"Embrace anyone who will embrace you," the colonel said.

"Initially I didn't agree with Col. MacFarland," Devlin said. "I said we shouldn't support this guy right off the bat, kind of ease into this.

"Maybe he's not the guy."

MacFarland would regularly say where you stand is where you sit. "The closer you were to them, the better you know them, the more you trust them," MacFarland said of Sattar and his allies. "The farther away you are, the more you're just reading these black-and-white intelligence reports on these guys' checkered pasts and you're saying, 'Hmm, I don't know about these guys.'"

MacFarland appreciated Devlin's views. He provided a detached assessment of Sattar that made the brigade think hard about jumping in bed with Sattar. "He would bring a lot of analysis to the discussion which I didn't have access to," MacFarland said. "I disagreed with him. I knew he was a pessimistic guy."

Devlin was unusual in the intelligence community. He wasn't afraid to make a prediction. Most intelligence officers will cover themselves by being so vague that any outcome will fit their analysis.

"Pete was my devil's advocate. He said Sattar was a thug. I did get that sense, but he was one of the honest criminals."

MacFarland had a different perspective. He was desperate for a solution. His soldiers were dying every day. Many of those fighting the Americans were not al-Qaeda and could be flipped. Sattar seemed like the solution.

"For the sake of my own sanity I had to believe all those losses will result in something positive," MacFarland said.

The popular notion of an Arab sheik is that of a warlord-type figure, like the Omar Sharif character in *Lawrence of Arabia*. In truth, they are shrewd businessmen, often overseeing vast enterprises. They are more comfortable cutting a deal in a back room than riding a horse into the desert leading a band of warriors—more Tammany Hall than desert warrior.

Sheiks are by nature a conservative, cautious bunch. They don't get ahead of their people. That's why so many were on the fence when the Ready First brigade showed up in Ramadi. The wealthy tribal leaders are secular and educated. But their people were drifting away from their influence. The Sunni populace in Anbar were nursing a deep resentment "to the foreign occupier who did nothing other than to turn upside down 1,300 years of a social arrangement in which the Sunnis ruled and the Shia are expected to be ruled," said James Soriano, a State Department official who was based in Ramadi.

When the powerful sheiks decamped for Amman and Dubai, radical imams back in Iraq were tapping into the resentment, drawing young men into the insurgency. There were few jobs or schooling opportunities. The insurgency grew and al-Qaeda was solidifying its hold on the western desert.

"Sheiks are not really leaders," Soriano said. "They're followers. They are very timid."

Under normal circumstances, charisma doesn't matter. Tribal leaders don't run for election. Most are selected by a tribal council in a process that is part nepotism and part merit. They succeed by distributing resources and taking care of their people. Most are large men who are most comfortable behind the scenes, negotiating and arbitrating disputes.

But these were not normal circumstances. Sattar, with his dark eyes, goatee, and sharp features, was made for television. He directly challenged the imams who were exploiting the disaffection.

"Clerics who preach politics are frauds," Sattar said.

Philosophically, the sheiks were in agreement. The extremists posed a threat to the sheiks' way of life. But the powerful sheiks weren't openly challenging that notion. That wasn't how they operated. It had been many generations since they had been called on to fight. Under Saddam, their survival had been mostly based on negotiation. The sheiks were dealing with both the Americans and al-Qaeda, hedging their bets.

Sattar was different. He stared into the camera and directly challenged the main spokesman for the Muslim Scholars Association, Sheik Harith al-Dhari. There was little that was scholarly about the organization. It provided a religious and political cover for the insurgency. Dhari was on Arab satellite television around the clock, criticizing the American occupation from his exile in Syria. He had largely remained unchallenged—until Sattar decided to take him on.

Sattar tried the same approach with the Iraqi Islamic Party, the main Sunni political group, which was also critical of the U.S. military and ambivalent about the "honorable resistance." Anbar's governor and most of the provincial council were members of that party. Sattar could challenge them in ways Americans couldn't. He taunted them on television for running to Baghdad to hold their meetings in the safety of the fortified Green Zone, home to the U.S. Embassy and other government offices.

Sattar's media blitz was little noted by the Americans at the time. It was playing out on Arab satellite networks.

He was not only taking on al-Qaeda. He was taking on the fence-sitting Sunni establishment. It was bringing Sattar notoriety. "Wars have a lot of ways of creating social circulation," Soriano said. "It turns society upside down.

"So a second-drawer sheikh is now in the top drawer."

———

There is nothing meandering about the Euphrates River as it flows through western Iraq. It cuts back and forth sharply between Ramadi and Syria, appearing on the map as the ragged teeth of a saw. For centuries tribes have controlled the smuggling routes that run along the river and into cosmopolitan, teeming Baghdad. Ramadi, with a population of about 400,000, is the largest and most important of the towns, villages, and cities nestled along the Euphrates.

By modern times, Ramadi had grown into a sprawling city, the key to Iraq's Sunni western desert. The cluster of downtown buildings gives way to large homes in the suburbs and finally to farms and date orchards along the river. Amid the sprawl are open industrial areas of factories and warehouses.

The city was born in 1869 of an attempt by the Ottomans to control the rowdy tribes of the Dulaime confederation in western Iraq. Even the Ottomans, whose hands-off style of running an empire involved a lot of delegation to the locals, felt the need to keep an eye on the tribes.

The British chose Ramadi to stage a magnificent tribal tribute to Faisal, the Sunni leader whom they had chosen to rule Iraq after World War I. On July 31, 1921, Faisal arrived by motorcar in Ramadi where he was greeted by hundreds of tribesmen gathered along the banks of the Euphrates. As Gertrude Bell, Britain's oriental secretary, approached the river she saw a black tribesman mounted on a white camel holding aloft the standard of the Dulaime. Bell watched Faisal take his place before the assembled tribesmen with a sense of pride.

"He was supremely happy—a great tribesman amongst famous tribes and, as I couldn't help feeling, a great Sunni among Sunnis," she wrote in a letter to her father.

The ceremony was engineered by Bell as part of her effort to build tribal support for Faisal before his coronation on August 23, 1921. Ali Sulaiman, the "sheik of sheiks," would lead the Dulaime tribes in pledging their allegiance to Faisal. If Faisal, who was born in present-day Saudi Arabia, was an odd choice to lead Iraq, Sulaiman was also not a perfect candidate to unite the tribes. The authentic paramount sheik among the Dulaime was Sheik Dhari ibn Dhakir. But he was implicated in the killing of a British officer, Col. Gerard Evelyn Leachman, which helped touch off the 1920 revolt against the British. That disqualified him. Instead, the British turned to Sulaiman, who headed the British-organized Camel Corps.

The British would later question their choice of Sulaiman, as it became clear he had less credibility among the tribes than originally supposed. But things went well that hot July afternoon. Faisal spoke and Sulaiman declared his loyalty to the incoming monarch. Sulaiman then brought up about forty or fifty sheiks to individually pledge support to Faisal. "They laid their hands in Faisal's and swore allegiance," Bell wrote. Then they ate. It took eight men to carry each platter, which held a small mountain of rice crowned by a whole roasted sheep.

To officers raised on Britain's colonial edges, the sheiks represented manly virtues and warrior spirit. They were a counterweight to the corrupting, decadent life of the city, home to artists, writers, and intellectuals. The sheiks were men of action, living the clean, simple life of the desert. They valued loyalty and a crude form of justice. It was a romantic notion, perhaps a bit quaint and out-of-date even back then, but it was firmly held. But the British were a little conflicted. There were many in the Foreign Office who viewed the sheiks as Americans did when they first entered Iraq: a throwback, an obstacle to modernity.

Pragmatism, in the end, would dictate that the British create a strategy to deal with the tribes. After the trauma of World War I, the British public wanted their boys home—not enmeshed in another colonial quagmire for which there was no quick solution. Yet the generals could scarcely be expected to keep a lid on things in Iraq with only about 60,000 foreign troops. A revolt, led mostly by Shiite tribes in 1920, drove home the difficulty of keeping a lid on Iraq with so few British troops. The generals figured using tribes (reinforced with some Indian army units dispatched to Iraq) would reduce the need for British troops, particularly in the desert, where supply lines were vulnerable to raids.

Throughout Iraq's history, tribes and the state existed in an often uneasy balance. Tribes and sheiks draw their power from the central government and yet they sometimes challenge that authority. The British noted this in the 1920s. Even "the paramount Shaikh depends on the backing of the central Government, without which he is powerless," colonial officials noted.

That gave the government leverage over the tribes, no matter who was in power. Saddam had his favorites and for the most part he successfully worked one against the other. After the Shiite uprising in 1991, Saddam relied even more heavily on family, clan, and tribe. He surrounded himself with cronies from his hometown of Tikrit, but also relied on the tribes and families in

Fallujah and Ramadi to staff the highest levels of his military and intelligence agencies. He supplied favored tribes with guns and ammunition.

Saddam excelled at keeping a lid on the tribes by manipulating tribal politics and rivalries to his advantage. Ramadi was always an explosive mix of tribal rivalries and backroom plotting. In 1995 it erupted in open revolt when Iraqi Air Force Gen. Mohammed Mazloum al-Dulaimi was arrested in November 1994 on suspicion of launching a coup against Saddam. His powerful family thought they had convinced Saddam to spare his life. Instead he was tortured and killed by Saddam's regime. His body was dumped at his family's compound in Ramadi.

In response, his brother, a brigadier general in a Republican Guard unit, launched an armored attack on the prison complex at Abu Ghraib, apparently in an effort to free hundreds of other members of the Dulaime tribe who were detained as part of the alleged coup. Other Republican Guard units blunted the assault and set their sights on Ramadi. The city was sealed off and electricity and water was cut. Saddam launched a purge of Dulaime officers from the armed forces, where they held key positions.

The Anbar tribes resorted to a common tactic. They began hijacking and looting trucks moving along roads in western Iraq. The revolt was short-lived and eventually petered out, probably through a combination of killing some enemies and bribing others.

The Abu Reisha tribe was concentrated in west Ramadi and for generations plied the smuggling routes in Iraq's western desert.

It was never a powerful tribe. In the early part of last century it blew its chance to boost its influence when it fought with the losing Turks against the British during World War I. Most tribes in the Dulaime federation backed the British. It was a point of pride to Sattar that his ancestors never abandoned the Turks even though it meant they were marginalized during the decades of British rule after World War I. It proved his loyalty couldn't be bought.

"The Turks lost and we never betrayed them," Sattar told Capt. Sean Frerking, an officer on Deane's staff.

"When we commit to a cause we go to the very end."

Lt. Gen. Graeme Lamb, a British officer who served as deputy commander of the Multi-National Force-Iraq, was taken by MacFarland to meet Sattar. The sheik launched into a long flowery speech about how honored he was to meet the general.

MacFarland turned to Sattar and said, "Tell General Lamb about your grandfather."

It was one of the few times Sattar appeared flustered. MacFarland suppressed a laugh.

"It was an honorable fight," Sattar blurted out.

Lamb, a veteran of Northern Ireland, knew that coalition commanders had to deal with all sorts of people, including those with unsavory backgrounds, if they wanted to get any traction in reconciling with the former enemy. These were the sort of people who knew where the bodies were buried, sometimes literally. Lamb was fond of pointing out to coalition colleagues that you reconcile with your enemies, not your friends.

Lamb was charmed by Sattar.

"He was a regular scallywag," Lamb said. "As the metropolitan police officer would say he had previous," this being British-speak for a prior record.

By the fall of 2006 it seemed that the Abu Risha, under Sattar's leadership, had made the right call this time. Sattar was rising to the occasion in ways that would have been impossible to predict based on his background as a mid-level smuggler with a reputation as a gunslinger. During a five-hour meeting with Sattar in October, MacFarland noticed he was interrupted three times to take calls from Prime Minister Nouri al-Maliki on his cell phone.

Sattar's growing prominence and outspoken challenges to al-Qaeda made him a target. At this stage of the Awakening, killing Sattar would spell the end of the movement. MacFarland ordered a tank to park permanently in the sheik's front yard.

14

The Chairman's Briefing

I regret that on my arrival in Mesopotamia I was too
much occupied with military matters, and too ill-
informed regarding the political problem to go among
the people with advantage.

—LT. GEN. SIR AYLMER L. HALDANE,
COMMANDER OF BRITISH FORCES IN IRAQ, 1920

Marine Gen. Pete Pace, chairman of the Joint Chiefs of
Staff, looked almost ashen when Col. Pete Devlin finished his brief. Pace was on one of his regular visits to Iraq and
was visiting the First Marine Expeditionary Force, headquartered at Camp Fallujah in Anbar Province. Devlin was assigned
to give Pace a routine intelligence briefing. Devlin gave him a
particularly blunt assessment of the situation in Anbar.

"At the rate we're going we're not going to militarily defeat
al-Qaeda," Devlin told Pace.

"We can continue to conduct raids until we're blue in the

face but the Iraqis themselves have to make a political decision to fight against al-Qaeda.

"He was really taken aback," Devlin recalled. "I really threw a bucket of water on him."

Devlin found himself feeling bad for Pace, who was under pressure in Washington. Retired generals had launched broadsides at his boss Rumsfeld and the Pentagon was coming under increasing criticism for the way it was fighting the war in Iraq. The White House had begun to cast about for a new strategy and was increasingly freezing Pace out of the discussions.

Pace thought for a second. He seemed to want reassurance.

"Okay, but we can't militarily lose to al-Qaeda either, in other words be thrown out of the province?"

Devlin assured him that couldn't happen.

Pace was a great marine with an unblemished record of forty years in the service. But he was struggling with the new type of war the United States was fighting. In Anbar, nearly the entire population opposed the U.S. presence or was intimidated into submission. In order to defeat al-Qaeda, the militants would have to be separated from the population.

Pace left the room shocked at what he had just heard. Devlin, a well-regarded intelligence officer wise in the ways of the military bureaucracy, knew he had to get a memo out quickly. Pace would be returning to the Pentagon soon and would be demanding answers from his staff. "I just briefed the chairman of the Joint Chiefs of Staff that the situation was pretty dang bad in Anbar, much worse than he thought it was," Devlin said. "He's going to start asking some questions about why he had to go to Anbar to find this out."

He called a colleague, Maj. Ben Connable, who was then at the Marine Corps Intelligence Activity in Quantico, Virginia, for help in turning his PowerPoint briefing into a memo. The officers posted the memo on a classified Web site. It was standard procedure. Other intelligence professionals could read it and comment or disagree. Most agreed with it.

Weeks later a story about the memo appeared on the front page of *The Washington Post*, under the headline, SITUATION CALLED DIRE IN WEST IRAQ; ANBAR IS LOST POLITICALLY, MARINE ANALYST SAYS.

It's not clear who leaked the memo, but not hard to figure out why. The front-page story was a direct assault on Rumsfeld's management of the war. "This is stick it right in the eye of the Department of Defense and Rumsfeld, to say you're not being honest with the way this war is going," Devlin said.

"That's why I think it was leaked."

In Ramadi, people were puzzled by the headline. There was plenty of violence in the city, but they were seeing progress. "It made me mad that people were out there dying every day and here's somebody saying, 'We lost,'" said Marine Maj. Teddy Gates.

Three days before the story appeared, Sattar had pledged his support to U.S. forces and the situation was getting a lot less dire. The presence of combat outposts, more Iraqi police recruits, and a growing number of friendly tribes were starting to have an impact.

But the debate in Washington seemed to continually lag about six months behind events on the ground in Iraq. The tide was turning in Ramadi, but it had little to do with decisions made or not made in Washington. The developments in Ramadi were happening under the radar.

Ramadi didn't fit the narrative shaped back in Washington. Critics were saying the war couldn't be won. It was a quagmire and a mistake. On the right, a growing number of influential conservatives were pushing for sending more American troops to Iraq to arrest the increased violence and to create an environment for political reconciliation.

Ramadi told a story somewhere in between. The United States had no overarching strategy, so commanders on the ground had a lot of latitude. Those with initiative could experiment. It was America's first entrepreneurial war. The Ramadi experiment was working.

"I had a lot of flexibility," MacFarland said.

"So I just ran with it. But I ran in a predetermined direction."

15

Shark Fin

The longer the tribal political system can be preserved the better . . .

—BRITISH POLITICAL OFFICER IN 1918

The call came on a satellite phone to Lt. Col. Chuck Ferry at about 3 P.M. on a November afternoon. "Al-Qaeda is up here!" a sheik yelled breathlessly into the phone.

"They are wiping my tribe out. They are killing my family. I need your help."

The man, who spoke to Ferry's interpreter, identified himself as Sheik Jassim from Sufia, a neighborhood in northeast Ramadi on a peninsula that juts into the Euphrates. The U.S. military called the area the Shark Fin.

Ferry was puzzled. His unit, the First Battalion, Ninth Infantry, had just arrived in east Ramadi as a replacement unit in MacFarland's brigade a month earlier. He didn't know a Sheik Jassim.

He called brigade headquarters on the other side of the city and requested drones over the location so he could see what was going on. He scrutinized the video downlink as it appeared on screens in his command post at Camp Corregidor, a base on Ramadi's east side. He saw a firefight, but couldn't distinguish friend from foe. A couple of homes were on fire. Men were running around shooting at each other. He ordered his interpreter to have the sheik use the GPS feature to get a fix on his location.

Ferry had spent most of the previous week planning for an operation scheduled to commence the following day in the Mala'ab area. It was a priority of his boss, Col. Sean MacFarland, who was currently on leave. Any military offensive to help the unknown sheik would certainly delay the planned operation, which was a critical part of the overall Ramadi campaign. The sheik's tribe, the Albu Soda, was squeezed into a tiny area called the Shark Fin, so named because of the way it jutted into the river.

It was a problem area for the Americans. Al-Qaeda regularly used the region to launch rockets and mortars into Camp Corregidor, the U.S. base in Camp Ramadi. The area wasn't a priority because it was isolated and could be contained until the Americans were ready to secure it. If Ferry mounted a rescue operation it would mean traversing streets that would be laced with roadside bombs. He had never heard of the sheik who was now asking him to risk his troops' lives for an area of limited value.

Ferry ordered his quick reaction force of tanks and infantry to get ready just in case.

He was a seasoned warrior with five combat tours, including one in Somalia. He had served eight years with the Rangers and was a former enlisted man in the Special Forces. His freshly arrived battalion was to begin clearing remaining pockets of al-Qaeda in the eastern parts of the city, as part of a methodical push to secure the rest of the city. Sattar and his allies had helped bring security to the city's west side, but large portions of the east were still in the hands of insurgents.

Sheik Jassim Muhammad Saleh al-Suwadawi was known to U.S. forces, though Ferry had not yet been briefed on him. A grizzled former Iraqi Army officer, Jassim had begun holding secret talks with Sattar weeks earlier. Under the cover of darkness he would sneak across the river on a small skiff and one of Sattar's entourage would pick him up and traverse the darkened roads north of the city to meet Sattar at his compound. At times he had to swim the river, once almost drowning. He had sold his last cow to purchase a Thuraya telephone so he could stay in touch with Sattar. Like Sattar, Jassim was not a prominent sheik. He assumed leadership of the Albu Soda tribe when the traditional sheik fled the country.

The brigade was squeezing al-Qaeda through the summer and into the fall. By November there were still pockets of al-Qaeda inside the city and in support bases in the east, just outside the city center. The Shark Fin was one such support base, where al-Qaeda had freedom of maneuver. Since the Americans weren't ready to secure the area, they responded to al-Qaeda mortar attacks by firing artillery back into the neighborhood. Jassim's neighborhood was getting pummeled by American artillery and he was getting shoved around by al-Qaeda.

By November, the sheik could see which way the city was going. He wanted to be out from underneath al-Qaeda's thumb.

One night, Sattar had gotten a message to Jassim, either by satellite telephone or by courier, that he wanted to see him. Lt. Col. Jim Lechner, MacFarland's deputy, met the sheik at Sattar's house and listened to his pitch.

"I need arms and equipment right now," Jassim told him.

Lechner was sympathetic, but he was a keen tactician and not one to make empty promises. The brigade just wasn't ready to secure the Shark Fin yet.

"We just couldn't do it," Lechner said. "I just couldn't guarantee to him right then that, yeah, we could put a U.S. company in his village."

Sattar's alliance was able to supply Jassim with a few rifles. Nothing more. "The enemy is behind you and the sea is in front of you," he was told. Jassim was told to hang on until help could come.

The sheik returned to his tribal area and put out the word that al-Qaeda would no longer be welcome there, with or without American help. He established a small force of seventeen men armed with AK-47s to protect the neighborhood. They would be no match for the much better equipped al-Qaeda.

Jassim then met with some of the al-Qaeda leaders in an effort to forestall violence until he could quietly build up his forces. The al-Qaeda leaders offered Jassim money if he would allow their militants to move through his tribal area. They met at a neutral sheik's home. Jassim brought five armed men with him. Unknown to him at the time, al-Qaeda had planned to kidnap and kill Jassim if he refused the offer. Jassim was noncommittal and left, with plans to reopen negotiations later. He was stalling for time.

Within a week, al-Qaeda killed a man from the neighboring Albu Mahal tribe, who were friends of Jassim's. He went back to confront al-Qaeda.

"You've opened another wound," Jassim told al-Qaeda's representatives. "We've just agreed that there will be no more killing. Therefore, no agreement, no peace with you. Period."

Al-Qaeda attacked the following day, November 25.

About forty to fifty al-Qaeda fighters arrived in a large parking lot in the center of the peninsula. They then split into three assault teams, using two roads and a canal to move northward into Jassim's neighborhood. The militants launched a barrage of mortars as they came north. Jassim had his seventeen men at four checkpoints in his neighborhood. They only had about thirty to forty rounds each for their AK-47s and they had one light machine gun. Al-Qaeda militants came with AK-47s, rocket-propelled grenades, and mortars.

Jassim's men initially fought back, shooting at the militants from rooftops. When they ran low on ammunition they withdrew northward into the tip of the Shark Fin, using small Motorola radios to communicate. Al-Qaeda fighters wearing ski masks and dressed in black swarmed through the neighborhood, using scorched-earth tactics. Militants torched Jassim's empty home and burned down another house that belonged to the sheik. They killed old men, women, and children, according to Jassim. They were firing at electric generators, killing sheep, and burning vehicles. They torched eleven vehicles that belonged to Jassim and his brothers. The attack showed signs of planning and coordination. Abu Ayoub al-Masri, the top al-Qaeda commander in Iraq, had helped plan it, signalling its importance to al-Qaeda. Losing Ramadi would be a blow.

Jassim's men attempted to make a last stand in a cluster of buildings that had clear fields of fire near the tip of the peninsula. There was nowhere else to go. Their backs were to the river.

Jassim continued to beg the Americans for help.

Ferry was in a tight spot. MacFarland wasn't around, he didn't know Sheik Jassim, the area was unknown and dangerous, and the brigade was counting on him to launch a major offensive in another area the following day. He called Lt. Col. V. J. Tedesco, the senior battalion commander, and Lechner, MacFarland's deputy, to seek guidance.

They both told him it was his call.

He ordered his men to mount up. Civilians were calling for help. Al-Qaeda was running roughshod over a neighborhood in his area of operations.

"I can't just ignore it," Ferry thought.

On the video in his command post there was still no way to tell al-Qaeda from the armed tribesmen, who were desperately trying to fend off the attackers. The sheik was told to order his men to wave towels or sheets above their heads in order to give the Americans a rough idea of where the tribe was located. He ordered F/A-18s to make low-level passes over the area in an effort to frighten off al-Qaeda. The warplanes screamed in a couple of hundred feet off the ground.

As Ferry moved north with infantry and tanks, his operations officer, Maj. Jared Norrell, was back in the battalion command post, monitoring the video feed from the drones. They could clearly make out four vehicles racing from the area dragging dead bodies that were chained or roped to the cars. Al-Qaeda's strategy was to intimidate the tribe with a blunt message: This is what happens to anyone who cooperates with the Americans or joins the Awakening.

The vehicles dragging the dead bodies were the only safe targets from the air. Ferry gave the okay to the pilots. Within minutes, three of the vehicles were blown up by F/A-18 attack aircraft and a fourth was hit by a hellfire missile fired from an unmanned Predator. The cars were obliterated, leaving between ten and twelve insurgents dead.

Most al-Qaeda were fleeing the area, scared off by the air strikes and the low-level flights. They hadn't expected the American response. One car full of militants was racing south and didn't see Ferry's darkened convoy moving up the road. The Americans had night vision goggles; the insurgents didn't. The Americans opened fire on the car with machine guns and small arms fire, killing several militants.

The road narrowed as Ferry's convoy of infantry and tanks approached the peninsula. There were canals on either side of the road, making the convoy vulnerable to ambush. The convoy neared the Sufia neighborhood when it encountered its first obstacle: half a dozen large palm trees cut down so they blocked the road. The trees were laced with roadside bombs. The normal procedure is to call for a bomb disposal unit to clear the obstacle, but Ferry figured there wasn't enough time. They were close enough now to see the glow from the fires that al-Qaeda was setting as they torched homes.

Ferry ordered his tanks to fire their 120mm main guns at

point-blank range into the obstacles. Infantrymen on foot then cleared ahead of the tanks and picked through the smoking debris to see if there were any remaining explosives. They rolled on until they encountered an obstacle just up the road and followed the same procedure.

Ferry's interpreter called the sheik and asked if he could hear the tanks.

He could. They were getting close.

Ferry ordered the sheik to light a bonfire in the middle of the road so that the Americans could identify the sheik as they approached the area. It was late fall and the evenings were getting cold. As the convoy rolled into the neighborhood, Ferry's men saw the exhausted tribesmen, wearing coats over their dishdashas, or long robes, and carrying AK-47s. Fires glowed throughout the neighborhood. Most of the militants had fled by then.

The sheik emerged from the darkness to greet Ferry, thanking him for coming to their rescue. Ferry launched into a series of questions to get a handle on the location of the sheik's tribe and any militants that might not have escaped. His troops got into a few small firefights but most al-Qaeda had left. The neighborhood was a mess. Most of the bodies had been removed from the road, but there were fires everywhere and streaks of blood on the pavement, where the tribesmen had been dragged through the streets.

Ferry and his men assessed the damages. Jassim said he lost seven of his fighters and another ten old men, women, and children. The Americans began treating the wounded.

The tribesmen needed blankets, heating oil, and food. They

also wanted weapons and ammunition in case al-Qaeda came back. Technically, the U.S. Army was not supposed to be arming tribes, but they couldn't leave the tribe twisting in the wind, at the mercy of al-Qaeda.

Ferry called Lechner at the brigade operations center. Within hours, Lechner and Patriquin were leading a convoy across the darkened city at 2 A.M. with a truckload of about a hundred AK-47s and fifty thousand rounds of ammunition. Jassim was estatic.

The sheik took Ferry aside and explained the situation. "If you Americans leave, al-Qaeda will come back and kill anyone left," the sheik told Ferry.

Ferry thought for a second. "If you're willing to pledge your tribe's allegiance and help me hunt down al-Qaeda, then I'm not leaving," he told him.

That night a company remained behind. The Americans stayed by the tribe for the next fifteen months of their deployment.

MacFarland's brigade had been following a strategy of allying with the tribes, but this was a step further. The Americans just handed a truckload of AK-47s to a tribe in the middle of the night. The brigade had chosen sides.

"It was the most direct support we had given a tribe," Lechner said. "We kind of snap-linked right into this tribe and sorted out the officiality of it afterwards."

It was typical of the Ready First's approach. They operated under broad guidelines, but they didn't use the rule book as a crutch. Previous units concluded it wasn't U.S. policy to "arm tribes." The policy hadn't changed, but MacFarland's commanders were encouraged to use their own initiative. MacFarland would take the heat if there was any.

Ferry wasn't sure how MacFarland would react, however. He had already briefed MacFarland on the planned Mala'ab operation before the commander had gone on leave. It was a major operation now sidetracked because of a call from a desperate sheik.

MacFarland returned less than a week later.

"You did exactly what I would have told you to do," MacFarland said, grinning.

He immediately launched into a discussion of how they would exploit the changes on the battlefield. Mala'ab could wait. The plan had changed. They would pursue al-Qaeda in Sufia, the Shark Fin area. Jassim had plenty of intelligence. Some of his tribesmen had worked for al-Qaeda as low-level fighters. They knew plenty. For the next six weeks they chased al-Qaeda in Sufia, mopping up al-Qaeda cells throughout the area.

Al-Qaeda militants had become ingrained in the neighborhood. Americans clashed with squad-size units (about twelve men) of insurgents as they fought to retake the area. Jassim was taken up in helicopters so he could point out al-Qaeda hideouts to U.S. Special Forces. He encouraged other tribes to join the Americans.

Navy SEALs were brought in to help train the new police recruits. Normally, the brigade would vet the police recruits before they entered the force. Now the brigade was having to conduct the vetting after it had already armed the tribe.

It was a bumpy process. Americans would show up for a joint patrol and find that an extra five names had been added to the target list.

"Who are these guys?" the Americans would ask. Some were simply rival tribesmen the Albu Soda hoped to rub out. The Americans fired some of the new recruits and carefully vetted target lists before they went on raids.

The decision to jump into the Sufia fight was done "without a lot of debate," said Capt. Niel Smith, a brigade staff officer who monitored the Shark Fin battle from the operations center.

"If we allowed this tribe to get murdered or intimidated it risked the whole thing falling apart," Smith said.

"How can we expect them to join our side if we can't protect them?"

16

Wisam

It was not, as is often supposed, by his individual
leadership of hordes of Bedouin that he achieved
success, but by the wise selection of tribal leaders.
—COL. PIERCE C. JOYCE
ON HIS COLLEAGUE T. E. LAWRENCE

A week after the Shark Fin battle, Patriquin and some other
brigade officers made one of their regular visits to Sattar's
compound. Sattar was outside his house in deep conversation
with a handful of sheiks when the Americans arrived. That wasn't
unusual. Sattar's compound had become the nerve center of a
tribal revolt that was spreading throughout Iraq's western desert.
It was usually buzzing with intrigue.

Patriquin took note of the men Sattar was huddling with.
They were from the Albu Aetha tribe, who lived in a region
north of the river that hadn't yet been secured. Patriquin had
never seen more than a couple of Aetha sheiks at a time. Now

there were five of them, discussing joining the Awakening with Sattar. Patriquin and Lechner weren't invited to join the discussion and didn't attempt to impose. They entered the house and waited for Sattar and Ahmad to finish the talks and join them.

After a few minutes Sattar entered the house, good-naturedly chastising Patriquin for staying away for so long. Sattar announced to Patriquin that he planned to marry a young woman from the Ali Jassim tribe across the river. Patriquin feigned surprise, saying Sattar was already married. Sattar said he was taking the extra wife in order to unite the tribes. He joked that his next wives would be American and British to complete the peace process. At tribal gatherings Sattar would address his counterparts flanked by an Iraqi and American flag.

The men then launched into a long discussion of recruiting. Hiring, training, and equipping police was a constant source of headaches. The police were recruited through their local tribes, but the Americans needed to ensure that they were paid and equipped by Iraq's Shiite-dominated government. The tribes wanted arms and money and constantly complained about not getting paid by the Interior Ministry. Lt. Col. Jim Lechner spent long hours sorting through the issues.

The brigade needed to support the tribes, but they had to do so within the overall U.S. policy of backing the central government. The brigade was masterful at walking this line. In order to give Sattar a boost, the brigade agreed to allow him to set up a militia of several thousand men who were not part of the regular police force. They wouldn't have to go to the police academy, which at the time was in Jordan, or pass the literacy tests, which were often a major obstacle to getting into the police. The brigade helped ensure that Iraq's Interior Ministry paid the salaries of Sattar's battalions, which were called Emergency Response Units. They built a force of several thousand men under Sattar's direct command.

"They're really just militia securing their homes but they're government militia," MacFarland said. "That was the key distinction."

They didn't look like much, but they fought aggressively. They converged on the scene with cars, trucks, and buses, spilling out of the vehicles in an odd assortment of uniforms. Some were former military and donned old Saddam-era Republican Guard uniforms.

"It looked like a 1920s era black-and-white Charlie Chaplin movie," said Marine Col. Steve Zotti, an Iraqi Army adviser. But they fought well, he said.

On one operation, Sattar was in the second vehicle in a small convoy that captured almost one hundred insurgents.

Sattar, Ahmad, and the Americans hashed over the recruiting issues, and just before lunch was served another large contingent of Iraqis arrived, including Sheik Abbas, who was involved in the Sufia fighting a week earlier. Abbas had regularly complained about the American presence. Now he smiled broadly and promised to send at least thirty police to the next recruiting drive. He boasted that his men killed four al-Qaeda in the past few days, saying the militants were caught trying to conduct a reconnaissance on his positions.

Things were going the way Patriquin had hoped. There was still some skepticism at the higher command, but that was melting away amid dramatic progress. At the heart of the success were the sheiks. Patriquin had been among the first to believe they could turn the tide of the war in Anbar—and perhaps extend it countrywide.

Patriquin was not the architect of the tribal strategy. But he spoke Arabic and understood the tribal dynamics probably better than anyone in the brigade. He and Lechner worked closely together, under MacFarland's broad guidance. They were an odd pair. Lechner pursued the tribes because it worked; it was an effective strategy. At heart, he was an infantryman focused on pursuing the enemy. He could be impatient and often demanding. Patriquin enjoyed the company of the sheiks. He knew their families. He barely finished high school but was an intellectual with a broad range of interests. He often bristled at conventional military discipline and rules. He grew a thick mustache and Sattar gave him the tribal name, "Wisam," or warrior. He spoke like them.

"You are the mujahedeen," the holy warriors, Patriquin would tell the sheiks when they gathered at Sattar's compound.

"You are the people's voice."

Before the Ready First left Germany for Iraq, Patriquin visited Capt. Russ Wagner, who was stationed in Weisbaden. Patriquin's official role with the brigade was civil affairs officer, meaning he would work on building government institutions and support the economy with civilian institutions. The two sat in Wagner's office and Patriquin launched into a discussion of what Wagner should read and study in preparation for his tour in Iraq. Patriquin enjoyed playing the role of mentor.

Patriquin said the United States wasn't talking to the right people. He said the U.S. military should buy loyalty first and then build on those relationships. The United States can't simply convince people to come over to its side because it represents freedom and democracy.

"You have to show them the benefit of coming to your side of the table," Patriquin told Wagner. "Once you get him to your side of the table then you can become friends." Wagner was impressed by the passion and power Patriquin brought to an argument.

Patriquin had earned a reputation as being a wise guy and a cutup. He chafed at staff meetings and PowerPoint briefings. When he was stationed at Fort Bragg he tooled around the base on a large Harley-Davidson that he had mostly built himself. He enjoyed the bad boy image.

"He was a bit of a rebel," Wagner said.

When he was a platoon leader in the Eighty-second Airborne at Fort Bragg he was often butting heads with his company commander, a more conventional-minded infantry officer.

"He had no problem telling battalion or brigade commanders, 'this is what you need to do.' Not just 'what I recommend.'"

"Tell me what you need done, not how to do it," he would tell his company commander. Even while planning field exercises, he would challenge his commander when the captain would default to a textbook solution of using overwhelming force to defeat the enemy. Patriquin believed speed, agility, and smarts often won over size.

When he had to bail out one of his soldiers from jail after getting in a fight in town, he would ask who won. "We're still going to punish you, but I just want to know if you can whip someone's ass."

Wagner and Patriquin were lieutenants with the Eighty-second Airborne Division in Fort Bragg, North Carolina, when al-Qaeda attacked New York and Washington on 9/11. When word of the attacks got out, the officers scrambled to get back to the command post on base, figuring their unit would soon be called up. The Eighty-second is light infantry, designed to be quickly deployed. The brigade that Wagner and Patriquin belonged to at the time was designated the quick response unit.

At the time, Patriquin had just returned from Ranger School where he had injured his knee, preventing him from completing the course. He was in a knee brace and was awaiting surgery. The division didn't get orders immediately, but the unit started preparing for war, figuring it would be called on soon. Patriquin's injured knee meant he couldn't deploy with his unit. It was devastating news.

When his unit went off to the National Training Center in Fort Irwin, California, for a month of training, Patriquin was stuck behind in a desk job. Another lieutenant was given his platoon. Patriquin spent the time studying Pashto. Then he called the Fifth Special Forces Group, which was heading to Afghanistan, and asked if they needed someone who could speak a local language.

Some of his Eighty-second Airborne colleagues thought he had gone too far. The military's attitude toward ambition and initiative is conflicted. Officers are supposed to exhibit initiative on the battlefield, but going outside the chain of command is frowned on. Patriquin was more interested in getting near the action than following conventions.

Some also worried that he was too anxious for war. He was married and at that time had two small children at home. "Why are you chomping at the bit so bad?" Wagner asked him.

Patriquin went to Afghanistan attached to Special Forces as an intelligence officer. In Afghanistan, Patriquin wore a beard and the loose-fitting clothes of the locals, like other Special Forces soldiers. At one point he found himself with a group of Tenth Mountain Division soldiers who were cut off from their officers.

"Hey, guys, you're not going to believe this," he told them. "Don't look at the beard. Don't look at the clothes. I'm actually a lieutenant in the Eighty-second Airborne.

"Anyone outrank me?" There was silence. "Okay, I'm in command now. " He led them into the fight.

Patriquin wanted to join the army since he was a child, "That's all he talked about," his father, Gary Patriquin, said. But his father insisted he graduate from high school first. When the 1991 Gulf War was beamed into living rooms across the country, that only made him more anxious to join.

Graduating was not a given. He was extremely bright, but didn't like classwork. He came home from high school one day with a report card with all Fs. His father went to speak with his teachers, who said he refused to complete homework, which was

50 percent of the grade. "Travis was just not going to do it," his father said. He would also skip classes a couple of days a week.

The family was living in Lockport, Illinois, after his father took a job there and had moved from St. Louis. After the trouble with school, Travis went back to the St. Louis area to live with his aunt and complete high school.

There, his teachers gave up on traditional classes and sent him to the library on a special independent study project. "He did enough to graduate," his father said. Because he was still seventeen, his father had to sign the papers allowing him to enlist.

Soldiers knocked on his door on the day he was supposed to report for processing. He had overslept.

"He wasn't what you would call the biggest morning person," his father said. Later in the day, some sailors came by. Apparently, he had signed up for the navy too.

The army was quick to note his intelligence and sent him to language school to learn Arabic and then to officer training. He later completed his college degree in the army. As an infantry officer he was expected to go to the grueling Ranger School even though it wasn't required. He made five attempts at Ranger School, but was plagued by knee and ankle injuries that kept him from completing it. "He's an ox and Ranger School is a joint twisting adventure," Wagner said. Even after getting a Bronze Star in Afghanistan, his failure to complete Ranger School would haunt him. "He was devastated," his father said.

In Iraq, Patriquin was bored by the routine work of staff meetings. Instead, he was always on the road, meeting with sheiks and learning everything he could about the tribes. "His view is he could do more good out running around talking to sheiks," said Lt. Col. Pete Lee, the brigade's executive officer. Lee would talk to Patriquin at night after he came back from a day roaming around and talking to the sheiks. He tried to get Patriquin to spend more time on staff work, but to little avail.

Some of the other staff officers grumbled because Patriquin was given such a free rein in hanging out with sheiks. "Some people would say, 'Travis just goes over [to the sheiks] to bullshit,'" Lechner said.

MacFarland was inclined to let Patriquin roam. "I like giving people like that a long leash," MacFarland said.

While Lechner would talk business with Sattar or one of his men, Patriquin would play with Sattar's young kids or strike up a conversation with another member of the sheik's entourage. "His personality just meshed with those guys perfectly," Lechner recalled.

"They loved him. He looked a lot like them. He had a great affable personality that they really warmed to.

"Travis and I would sit down before we went in and we would map out how we wanted the whole visit to go. . . . The whole time I'm working out the details, Travis is kind of whispering in Sattar's ear, 'Hey, we kinda need this.'"

Patriquin read deeply into Arab culture. He was a rarity among Americans in Iraq in that he could see events from a tribal perspective. He understood that the Awakening was driven by the tribes. It was not an American creation, but the United States could easily blow it if it wasn't nurtured properly.

In early December, Patriquin was at Sattar's compound talking to one of his nephews, a twenty-five-year-old who served as

Sattar's bodyguard and was part of the sheik's inner circle. Most of the young men who joined the police in recent months were former insurgents, the man told Patriquin. "This confirms some suspicions about the area that I've had since we arrived, namely that when we arrived the only growth industry in Ramadi for a young man to get ahead in was terrorism, and that the average Iraqi eighteen-year-old looking for a life of adventure was far more likely to join the insurgency than the ISF [Iraqi Security Forces]," Patriquin wrote in a report later that day. Patriquin concluded that the young men viewed the police as a way "to serve their families, their country, and their tribes, which is in line with Arab idealism and doesn't compromise their belief system."

Patriquin understood that the young police recruits believed they were still fighting a foreign invader, but it was al-Qaeda—not the Americans. They were happy about switching allegiances. "Having fought us for years, they respect our military prowess, and are now very happy that we're all on the same side," Patriquin wrote. "The bulk of these young men were 'foot soldiers' and not very vested in the ideology of the insurgency anyway, and the promise of a life of adventure, steady pay, and being on the side of righteousness has proved to be the right mix" to get them to switch sides.

Patriquin would bristle when fellow officers dredged up complaints about Sattar's past or referred to the traditional sheiks in exile. "Patriquin would say, 'Hey, this guy's here and he's showing more loyalty to his people.'"

His stick figure PowerPoint demonstration was typical. It got to the core of the issue, but was also flippant. "He was visionary, very cantankerous, profane, obstructionist," according to Marine Maj. John Church, a civil affairs officer who admired him for all those traits.

One day Patriquin strode into the daily battle update briefing carrying a megaphone. It was the battery-operated type that made his voice robotic-sounding. It was used by the military to address large crowds. Speaking through the megaphone, Patriquin launched into a dead-on imitation of a Borg on *Star Trek*. "Resistance is futile. You will be assimilated."

The staff looked nervously at MacFarland who sat at the end of the table. MacFarland wore a bemused smile. The staff began cracking up.

"It was the kind of thing that only Travis could get away with," said Maj. Michael Wood, the brigade chaplain.

His blunt talk and irreverence was sometimes read as impertinence by more conventionally minded officers. It didn't sit well with Patriquin when these officers would attempt to provide guidance about tribes. He received an e-mail once from a marine colonel who referred to an oft-used reference from T. E. Lawrence suggesting that some matters are better left to the locals to sort out. The quote was often used to rationalize neglecting the tribes, allowing them to fend for themselves.

It wasn't in Patriquin's nature to let the e-mail go without a pithy response.

"Travis is, like, 'who is this guy?'" Church said.

Inevitably, Church would get an angry e-mail about the army captain who is dismissing his suggestions. "Doesn't this guy know he's addressing a lieutenant colonel in the Marine Corps?"

"I'll talk to him," Church would promise. "And I'd let it go."

Church was used to the complaints and they developed a routine. "'Hey, Travis, give me your wrist.' He'd hold it out and I'd slap it and say, 'Please don't do that again.'"

"He has the tendency to rub people who are not really confident in what they are doing the wrong way," Church says.

At a meeting with a State Department official at Camp Fallujah, Patriquin gave a briefing on the security situation in Ramadi and the brigade's tribal strategy. The higher headquarters at Camp Fallujah worried that recruiting police through the tribes could backfire. "The question was, why are we investing so much time and energy in recruiting these guys when they're just going to turn against us when we leave?" Church recalled. Patriquin's response was, "You can question all you want but we're doing it," said Church, who was at the meeting.

Patriquin had access to his own Humvee and had authority to visit almost anyone he wanted. "I don't want to say he had carte blanche from MacFarland, but he certainly had overhead cover," Church said, meaning MacFarland would defend Patriquin against bureaucratic sniping.

Staff officers for the Marine Expeditionary Force headquarters complained that Patriquin was freelancing. "They thought he was getting taken in and getting played for a sucker," MacFarland said.

"He wasn't. He was a very smart guy and knew what he was doing."

The freelancing paid off. At staff meetings, Patriquin would lean back in his chair, stare up at the ceiling, and absentmindedly swirl his laser pointer. "He would always just astonish you with his knowledge of your AO," said Bradley, referring to area of operations. "He knew all the people there and in more detail than we knew. The president of the university, the tribal sheik in this neighborhood, the demographics, where the marketplace was, how people in this neighborhood feel about the Iraqi Army. He was usually right."

The American public remained skeptical of the Iraq War, however. Casualties were high in the fall and winter of 2006. The signs of progress—police on the street and a shift in popular sentiment—is much harder to measure. "My measure of effectiveness would not be low friendly casualties," MacFarland said. "My measure of success would be defeating the enemy. Casualties, I couldn't let stop me."

The soldiers in Ramadi could feel the ground shift. "While there was still a long way to go, Travis knew—we knew—that we were going to win," Lechner said.

"We knew once you bring police into a neighborhood it's over," Lechner said. "It's done. It's just a matter of weeks, maybe even days.

"We were so deep into the city, we had so many police in the pipeline. Prime Minister Maliki was calling Sheik Sattar on the cell phone.

"We knew at least in Ramadi we were going to win."

17

Justice

[The tribes] are beginning to forget their former pred-
atory habits and take up the more peaceful pursuits
which flourish under a settled administration.
—BRITISH ADMINISTRATIVE REPORT, CIRCA 1919

L t. Col. Jim Lechner saw the bomb in time.

He was leading a small convoy down Route Sunset toward Combat Outpost Falcon to drop off two *Newsweek* journalists. The pressure plate IED lay across their path. He screamed
to his driver and shouted in the radio, "Plate in the road! Turn
left!"

The driver swerved, narrowly missing the bomb.

Patriquin and Marine Maj. Megan McClung, the brigade's
public affairs officer, were traveling in the Humvee right behind
Lechner. Their driver either didn't hear the warning or couldn't
swerve in time. The bomb went off underneath their vehicle,
igniting the gas tank and engulfing the Humvee in flames.

MacFarland was in the combat operations center when the report of the roadside bomb came in. Maj. Niel Smith handed the colonel a paper. MacFarland stared at the names of the KIAs. Patriquin, McClung, and Spec. Vincent Pomante, the gunner on the Humvee, had been killed instantly. The colonel asked Smith to confirm the report. Maybe it was wrong. MacFarland had been to a lot of memorial services. Almost nightly he went to the landing zone, where the bodies of his soldiers were encased in plastic shrouds and loaded into waiting helicopters. He was able to grieve and move on. He had no choice.

Smith came back with confirmation.

MacFarland wandered down the hall to his office. McClung was an energetic young marine officer who had been his media adviser. Pomante was a bright soldier who worked in the brigade's operations shop. Patriquin was a friend—a maverick who reminded MacFarland of himself as a young officer. All were members of his staff. He rushed over to Charlie Med, where the dead and injured were brought. Bradleys and Humvees were racing to the hospital. Soldiers jumped from vehicles and injured troops were carried into the hospital. MacFarland was off to the side, watching the chaotic scene, as he had countless times before. This time grief was accompanied by frustration and anger. He broke down.

Maj. Michael Wood, the brigade chaplain and a Baptist, saw MacFarland and quietly went over to speak with Navy Cmdr. Dennis Rocheford, a former enlisted marine who had served in Vietnam before becoming a Catholic priest and navy chaplain. The two chaplains had rushed to the hospital when they had heard there were casualties.

"Father, you need to go to the colonel," Wood told him.

That evening Lechner went to Sattar's house to break the news to him. Patriquin was Sattar's close friend and the sheik was also fond of McClung, a spirited marine officer who ran triathlons. Sattar greeted Lechner as he climbed out of his Humvee. Sattar had already heard of the deaths. He was in tears and Lechner could tell he had been drinking.

"Why do you Americans have to go out and fight and die?" Sattar asked.

"I wished Wisam had not gone out," he said using the tribal name the sheiks had given Patriquin.

"I'm going to find the people who did it."

It was the first U.S. memorial service attended by a large contingent of sheiks. They sat near the front, dressed in tribal robes and headdresses among hundreds of American soldiers who had come to pay their respects. At the front of the large dining hall were photos of Patriquin, McClung, and Pomante. In the photo, Patriquin sported a thick mustache and a wide grin. Next to the photos were M-16s, with their barrels pointed down and dog tags hanging from the pistol grip of each weapon. A pair of empty boots sat in front of each rifle.

MacFarland, looking drawn, walked to the lectern. He began to speak, but choked up. "We are left to carry on without them. Not an easy thing to do."

He talked about Patriquin's contribution. "When the history of this conflict is read, his name will loom large."

Then he referred to the final scene in *Saving Private Ryan*. "We here in Ramadi never need to wonder if we earned this sacrifice because we can earn it by fighting the good fight. And when that fighting is done, by living a good life."

Sattar, dressed in a jet-black robe and red-and-white-checked kaffiyeh, or head scarf, was among the first to come to pay respects after the eulogies. He stood in front of the photos with his hands outstretched and his palms up in the Islamic style of prayer. He reached out and clutched each set of dog tags briefly before returning to his seat.

MacFarland struggled to keep his composure through the ceremony but succumbed as he watched Sattar and others walk to the front and pay their final respects. A large marine major came up to MacFarland, buried his face in his chest, and cried. By then MacFarland's composure had returned. He had finished grieving inside. Amazing how that works, MacFarland thought.

Later that night, MacFarland was in the command post when a drone picked up images of a team of insurgents burying a roadside bomb. The brigade staff called in F/A-18 attack planes, which swooped in and strafed them with 20mm cannons. The survivors staggered off, seeking to escape, but the drone tracked them to another hiding place. The jets fired a Maverick missile at them, while the unmanned aircraft videotaped the attack.

"Watching them die felt good," MacFarland thought.

Less than twenty-four hours after the deadly roadside bomb, Lechner was over at Sattar's compound.

"We know who did it," Sattar said.

Sattar had a cousin who lived a block from where the convoy ran over the IED. He knew all about the attack.

For Lechner, this was personal. If it was a U.S. operation, the suspects would be held on criminal charges and released if there wasn't solid evidence. Anbar had no court system to speak of and gathering evidence in combat was next to impossible. U.S. soldiers called the system "catch and release."

If it was an Iraqi operation, Lechner figured odds were better that justice would be served.

"I didn't want American limitations and impediments to get involved in this," Lechner said. "I wanted to make sure this was done right. I wanted to make sure we maximized this and exploited it. I didn't want any American administrative bullshit involved in this."

The police chief responsible for that section of the city was Lt. Col. Salaam abu Alwani, a grizzled street fighter who the marines had been working with in Ramadi's city center. He liked to wear a ski mask and operate at night. Salaam was typical of many of the people who were enthusiastically working with the Americans now. He was a former Republican Guard officer who had the job of keeping the Anbar tribes in line for Saddam.

He took up smuggling with Sattar and had to flee to Saudi Arabia for two years. His intelligence was so unerring that the Americans assumed he had been an insurgent. He was systematically gutting the al-Qaeda cells on the west side of Ramadi.

"You have a smart brain," Salaam told Lechner when the two met. But, he said, "You don't understand my streets.

"Let's work together," Salaam said, breaking into a broad grin.

Sterling Jensen, who was interpreting on the mission, turned to Lechner. "This guy is the real deal."

Salaam did know what he was doing. A couple of Salaam's police knew the suspects, who were brothers. They had gone to school together. The police were ordered to go undercover and approach the brothers, Faris and Mohammed Talaa.

"We hear you got some Americans," one of the police said to the brothers.

The brothers made no effort to deny it. The suspects may have known the men were police, but they figured they grew up together. They wouldn't turn them into the Americans or Iraqi authorities. What the suspects didn't know is how much had changed since the sheiks started working with the Americans. The brothers had killed Americans who were friends with Sattar. The old rules no longer applied.

"Want to come see the video?" they asked the police.

Insurgents almost always taped attacks. It was a way of proving to their paymasters that they had completed their job and it also made good propaganda, posted to the Internet. The two young men showed the video on their computer to the undercover police.

The police learned that the brothers didn't sleep at home, possibly because they were on the run. So the police spoke to some relatives over tea, and determined where they stayed.

They had the intelligence they needed. They planned to execute the raid on December 19, twelve days after Patriquin, McClung and Pomante were killed. Lechner brought along about twelve Americans, his personal security detail. They met after midnight with Salaam and about twenty of his police. Lechner warned American marines and soldiers operating in the area that they would be conducting a low-profile operation downtown. They would likely not need American assistance.

The raiding party left a small U.S. outpost at about 1 A.M., quietly creeping down the dark streets of downtown Ramadi. The Americans were kitted out in their full protective gear and peered through night vision goggles. The Iraqis were dressed in a hodgepodge of uniforms, civilian clothes, and ski masks. Lechner was surprised at the proficiency of Salaam's men, many of whom were in their late teens or early twenties. These were street guys, some of whom probably previously worked as insurgents. When they came to a gate, they quickly and quietly removed the hinges so the door wouldn't squeak and warn the occupants before entering the courtyard.

They arrived at the target house at about 2 A.M. The police entered and went right to the bedroom and found one of the brothers asleep in a dishdasha. The police shined a flashlight in his face and pulled him out of bed by the hair, dragging him into the hallway. They recognized him. "Are you Mohammed Talaa?"

"Yes, I am."

"Where's your brother?"

"He's down the road."

Mohammed led the police to his brother, who was several houses away. They woke a young man who looked to be about eighteen. He was startled and had acne medicine spread on his face.

The police brought the two to a small detention facility in

Sattar's compound. There were a couple of police on duty to sign the suspects in. As they were writing the names down, Salaam came in with his ski mask on.

The initial shock had worn off and now the suspects appeared scared. They readily acknowledged to Salaam that they placed the IED.

Jensen started the night thirsting for revenge. He and Patriquin were close. Now he was looking at two frightened kids. "What am I supposed to think of all this?

"I don't feel like I want to get a pistol and shoot these guys even though they killed three of the people I worked with. I just thought, That's too bad. This is stupid. They got caught up for a hundred bucks or whatever it was."

Jensen and Lechner were impressed by how efficient the local police were. They had done what Americans could never do. After they grabbed the brothers, the police detained another eight men involved in the cell that placed the IED. The SEALs captured the cell leader in a separate raid that same evening.

"They know everybody," Lechner said. "They went to high school with all these cats. And so they just go and talk with their high school buds, they find out who the cell was, who was running it, all the names, wrapped them all up in thirty minutes."

"I've been on tons of raids when the Americans do it," Jensen said. "It's like the circus is coming to town. You ask, 'Where is so and so?'

"'I don't know. I haven't seen the person in five years.'"

The police under Sattar's control held the men for about two months. They confessed and signed statements about their involvement in planting the IED. It turned out they were unemployed kids who were paid about $500 to kill the Americans.

It occurred to Lechner that they could have just as easily signed up for the police. They had no ideology. It was about money.

The police had all the evidence they needed. One day, Lechner, Sattar, and Sattar's brother, Ahmad, were at Sattar's compound discussing the case. "What do you think we should do?" Sattar asked.

Lechner was a little surprised, figuring the Iraqis would want to take care of it themselves.

One of the brothers, Lechner does not recall if it was Sattar or Ahmad, said, "Sharia law is an option."

He elaborated: "We can execute them."

It put Lechner on the spot. Not only was the U.S. military required to build criminal cases against the suspects, but the American high command was putting similar pressure on the Iraqis so prisoners weren't languishing in prisons. To Lechner, it was a bit of a catch-22. Anbar had virtually no legal system with which to try suspects. Telling the Iraqis to try suspects in court was tantamount to sending them out the door.

Lechner agreed to transfer the suspects to U.S. custody. "If the three of us had been king for a day, we would've known exactly what we would have done," Lechner said.

"But when these lawyers start coming down from higher headquarters . . . I'm afraid to know what happened. They probably got released."

Jensen thinks the Americans misunderstand the Iraqis' sense

of justice. Iraqis generally won't beat a suspect unless they think he's lying.

"The Americans assumed . . . Sattar is going to be so ticked off at this guy because he loves Patriquin and he's going to kill them," Jensen said.

"If you've got a guy who killed a hundred people, but they say, 'Yes, I killed a hundred people. I did it because of this and this and this,' and it sounds reasonable to an Iraqi, the Iraqi is going to say, 'Okay, you're mine now. You work for me now.'

"But you get a guy who knows something and the Iraqis think that he's lying, they'll hit him and say, 'Why are you lying?'

"I think they have a finer sense of justice than we do. They've had to fight for justice."

18

Worthy Allies

When they began to think of us as reliable partners,
their attitudes began to change.

—COL. SEAN MACFARLAND

At midnight on December 31, 2006, MacFarland ordered the field artillery unit at Camp Ramadi to fire a single illumination round from a 155mm howitzer to mark the new year. The shell popped open high over Ramadi, casting a dim yellowish glow over the darkened city. Shadows shimmered and jumped as the shell descended slowly, swinging under its small parachute.

MacFarland kept a map that located the tribes in Ramadi and identified them by color. Green was friendly, yellow was ambivalent, and red, hostile. By January 2007, more than half the map was green. The red and yellow areas were limited to a shrinking corner in the south and east of the city. In late January, the brigade had gone an entire month without a soldier killed by a roadside bomb. U.S. Special Forces started shifting their efforts from Anbar to Afghanistan, since al-Qaeda in Ramadi was in disarray. The U.S. military didn't like talking about the numbers of enemy killed. It sounded too much like the discredited body counts of Vietnam. But the brigade did track those numbers. By January, they were killing fifty-five enemy for every friendly KIA. That didn't include whatever damage the tribes were independently inflicting on al-Qaeda or insurgents who refused to switch sides. The brigade was responsible for killing more than 1,100 insurgents and capturing another 1,200 by February 2007.

In the United States, the strong Democratic showing in midterm elections in November was a blow to the White House. The Iraq War was at the heart of much of the voter dissatisfaction. Immediately afterward President Bush said he had accepted the resignation of Defense Secretary Donald Rumsfeld. Robert Gates was named to replace him. Rumsfeld was an architect of the war and took most of the blame for what went wrong. Now the administration needed to figure out a new strategy.

Jack Keane, a retired four-star general, had teamed up with Fred Kagan, a strategist and military historian, and were meeting with officials at the White House, pushing a plan that would come to be known as the surge. Gen. Peter Pace, the chairman of the Joint Chiefs, was largely frozen out of the process and Bush was losing faith in Gen. George Casey, the man he approved to lead U.S. forces in Iraq. The new strategy pushed by Keane and Kagan, and supported by many within the military, was to increase the number of U.S. forces in Iraq and shift the emphasis from one of transitioning responsibility to Iraqi security forces to protecting the population.

If there were lessons to be gleaned from the remarkable changes in Ramadi they were lost amid the turbulent politics in Washington. Months before the surge, MacFarland's brigade was already employing the counterinsurgency principles that the new surge strategy would embrace. The Ready First had established eighteen combat outposts throughout the city while forming an enduring alliance with the tribes.

But Ramadi's turnaround was mostly invisible. When visitors from the United States included a trip to Ramadi on their schedule they were invariably surprised by what they found there. A top-level CIA official visited Ramadi in January and on the spot agreed to have the agency fund extra pay for police who agreed to leave their tribal area and work inside the city.

The public debate in Washington centered on troop levels in Iraq—not on how they should be deployed once there. On December 14, Senator John McCain came to Ramadi as part of a congressional delegation touring Iraq. They too were surprised about the developments in the city. The news most Americans were getting still painted Ramadi as a dangerous place. It wasn't completely secure, but the progress there was undeniable and instructive for those who cared to study it.

McCain, a Republican presidential candidate, was behind the surge strategy and had been sharply critical of Rumsfeld.

The Iraq visit amounted to a campaign appearance, *The New York Times* noted. The surge would become the centerpiece of his campaign. At a press conference in Baghdad right before he flew to Ramadi, McCain said that a substantial U.S. troop increase was under discussion by top U.S. commanders.

"Do you need more troops?" McCain asked MacFarland when he arrived in Ramadi.

MacFarland was blunt. He said they had enough forces and were making progress. More troops would help, but would be only a temporary solution. The key, MacFarland told McCain, was more Iraqi security forces. MacFarland put in a pitch for some help in clearing bureaucratic hurdles to speed the delivery of trucks and other supplies to the rapidly expanding Iraqi police.

"What we really need is assistance getting the Iraqi security forces built up faster," MacFarland told him.

"The police are going to win this. The faster we build 'em the faster we'll win."

McCain pressed him. "Yeah, but don't you think more troops would help the situation—more U.S. troops?"

MacFarland said there were enough American troops in Ramadi.

McCain, who has a famously sharp temper, grew irritated.

"You've been trying this approach since '04," McCain snapped. "It hasn't worked, my friend. What you need is more troops."

"It was very obvious by his demeanor that there was no discussion on it," recalled Lechner.

The senators were sitting around a plywood table in a conference room in the brigade headquarters. McCain was accompanied by Joe Lieberman, an Independent, and three fellow Republicans, Lindsay Graham of South Carolina, John Thune of South Dakota, and Susan Collins of Maine. They were all supporters of the war, although Collins said she had not yet made up her mind about a troop increase.

McCain told the officers he wanted to visit the government center. The room grew quiet. The press had painted the government center as a Fort Apache, where a group of heavily armed marines were surrounded by al-Qaeda militants. Security had gotten a lot better lately, but it was still dangerous. Taking a presidential contender and other senators into the center of Ramadi was just too risky, particularly without advance notice so that additional security could be established. Lt. Col. Pete Lee, MacFarland's executive officer, thought the senator was making the request to prove a political point. *If it's so secure here how about taking us to the most dangerous part of the city?*

Marine Maj. Gen. Richard Zilmer stepped in. "Sir, we're not going to do it today."

As the delegation was leaving, an officer buttonholed Lieberman. "Sir, I regret that I did not have the chance to speak in the meeting, but I want you to know on behalf of the soldiers in my unit and myself that we believe in why we are fighting here and we want to finish this fight. We know we can win it."

McCain caught some flak during the campaign from critics who suggested—in retrospect—that the turnaround in Ramadi proved that the country would have improved without the extra troops. CBS's Katie Couric asked McCain in July 2008 about a charge from Senator Barack Obama that some of the security improvements in Iraq could be traced to the Anbar Awakening and a decision by al-Maliki to crack down on Shiite militias. Obama "says that there might have been improved security even without the surge," Couric said.

"I don't know how you respond to something that is such a false depiction of what actually happened," McCain said. "Col. MacFarland was contacted by one of the major Sunni sheiks. Because of the surge we were able to go out and protect that sheik and others. And it began the Anbar Awakening. I mean, that's just a matter of history."

A week later Graham weighed in as the presidential race heated up. He got at the core of MacFarland's success without trying to tie it to the surge.

"One of the defining moments in turning Iraq around was in Anbar Province," he told a Washington news conference. "Sheik Sattar came to Col. MacFarland and said, 'We've had it with al-Qaeda in Anbar. They're brutal, they're making life miserable for us and we don't want to live under their thumb.'

"So this colonel seized the moment. He talked with the sheik and sent a tank and some American forces to surround the sheik's home.

"Some would have said no to the sheik, not given him the additional protection that he needed.

"And I think history would have recorded that decision poorly."

It wasn't entirely surprising that the public and politicians were unable to absorb the lessons of Ramadi. As late as January 2,

2007, a headline in *The Baltimore Sun* read: MARINES LOCKED IN
ANBAR STANDOFF. It was datelined Ramadi. The twenty-four-
hour news media was consistently behind developments on the
ground. Television is beholden to images. Explosions and violence draw cameras. In a conventional war, the military can always point to ground gained as a way to show progress. Those
rules don't apply in an insurgency, where the battle is for "human
terrain."

The insurgents have a large advantage in influencing media
coverage. One roadside bomb will draw more coverage than any
other measure of progress. As long as the insurgents can blow
things up occasionally they will hold the edge in the information war, arguably the most important front in an insurgency.
These kinds of wars will be won or lost based on perceptions—
not tactical victories.

Television, and even newspapers, had trouble seeing important but intangible developments as they were happening. Violence was more visible. Insurgents had mastered the war for
perceptions. They always videotaped their attacks on American
forces and established media cells that were responsible for post-
ing videos and statements on the Internet. In October 2006,
insurgents broadcast a video of a parade through downtown
Ramadi, showing masked gunman brandishing weapons and
hanging out of cars and on the backs of motorcycles. It was only
about six motorcycles, four cars, and a dozen or so insurgents.
But the video was run on a continuous loop on television so it
looked like a lot more. It gave the impression that the insurgents
were running the city. Brigade officers got an urgent call from

their higher headquarters when the video started airing on CNN and elsewhere.

Capt. Niel Smith took the call. "Do you know there is an al-Qaeda parade downtown?" he was asked. Smith said he didn't, but sent some drones overhead. It was in the Qatana area of downtown Ramadi. They saw nothing. Insurgents had dashed into the streets and demonstrated for the cameras and as quickly disappeared. It was aired regularly on cable news. The American officers dubbed it the "al-Qaeda Pride Parade."

Ramadi was much safer by December 2006, but it was the deadliest month for the brigade: fourteen American soldiers were killed. Casualties were often a lagging indicator, making it even more difficult to convince the public of progress.

In a Pentagon press briefing in January 2007, Zilmer confronted a skeptical Washington press corps. "On the matter of sheiks cooperating, we've heard that a couple times before," one reporter said.

"What makes you think that this one is different or that this time it will stick?"

Zilmer pointed to the large number of police recruits the sheiks were bringing in and other trends. Skepticism was warranted. The public had been fed these numbers before. In the early days of the war, the U.S. military was breathlessly reporting thousands of trained and equipped security forces on the rolls. Many of them melted away when confronted with fighting in Najaf and Fallujah in 2004. The army and police only looked impressive on paper.

The tipping point in Ramadi was invisible. The change was

happening in the hearts and minds of people who were sick of being brutalized by al-Qaeda and who came to trust a group of Americans who were living among them.

Some hints of the remarkable developments were, however, filtering back to Washington. Representatives of the State Department and the CIA sent cables or spoke to officials in Washington.

On the morning of Monday, December 11, President Bush went to the State Department to meet with officials involved in the reconstruction of Iraq. Bush had yet to announce his new strategy in Iraq. Jim Soriano, the State Department representative in Anbar, came up on the secure video to brief Bush.

"I can't tell you exactly what it is, but something is going on out here in Anbar. Things are starting to turn."

Bush seized on the bit of good news. Soriano was a cautious diplomat and early skeptic of Sattar. But he was beginning to change his mind. The CIA in Anbar had also sent a report back to Langley, highlighting the progress in Ramadi.

There were others who noted the significance of the changes in Ramadi: Lt. Gen. Stanley McChrystal, who commanded all U.S. special operations forces in Iraq and Afghanistan, could see MacFarland was on to something.

"Just keep driving on," he told MacFarland during a visit to Ramadi. "Fortune favors the bold."

The brigade had a breakthrough within their own chain of command in September during a visit by the corps commander, Lt. Gen. Peter Chiarelli. MacFarland laid out the astronomical growth in local police and how violence in some areas was dropping dramatically. He said talking to the brigade was like a "jolt of adrenaline." He talked it up back in Baghdad at corps head-quarters.

It wasn't until Gen. David Petraeus arrived with a new mandate and strategy, however, that the lessons learned in Ramadi were applied throughout the country.

Winning hearts and minds is a misleading phrase. The Ready First brigade hadn't convinced the Iraqis and their tribal leaders that the U.S. side was right. It had convinced the Iraqis that the Americans were winning. Changing sides would be in their best interest. In the tribal culture there is no shame in that. They do it all the time.

"Instead of telling them that we would leave soon and they must assume responsibility for their own security, we told them that we would stay as long as necessary to defeat the terrorists," MacFarland said.

"That was the message they had been waiting to hear.

"As long as they perceived us as mere interlopers, they dared not throw in their lot with ours. When they began to think of us as reliable partners, their attitudes began to change. Still, we had to prove that we meant what we were saying."

The way MacFarland saw it, the Americans had to prove *themselves* as worthy allies.

MacFarland and Sattar took a chance on each other. Both knew the stakes and neither entered the relationship with any illusions. They were odd partners: a devout Catholic from upstate New York and an Arab smuggler with a taste for whiskey. When they locked their hands together and raised them for a snapshot on September 9 they did as much to shift the tide in Iraq as any other single event.

In January, MacFarland told a visiting reporter that Ramadi "passed a turning point," though few had recognized it.

"Soon, everyone will," he said.

19

The Test

Go find me someone in Anbar Province at that particular moment who wasn't smuggling. Go find me somebody who had never been involved in criminal activities. The answer was there wasn't anybody.
—JOHN ALLEN, BRIGADIER GENERAL, USMC

In early 2007, Gen. David Petraeus arrived in Iraq with orders to overhaul U.S. strategy. Petraeus, who was renowned for his network of contacts throughout the U.S. Army, had heard about Ramadi, where against all odds a U.S. brigade had teamed up with sheiks and taken the city back from al-Qaeda. He wanted to learn more.

And Petraeus wanted to put Sattar to the test. Lt. Col. Jim Lechner was dispatched to ask Sattar to provide four hundred men for the Iraqi Army. Recruiting for the police directly benefited Sattar, since it meant local security and more influence for the sheik. The army was different. Soldiers could be deployed elsewhere in Iraq if needed. There was no direct benefit for the sheik.

Lechner arrived at the sheik's compound and after cigarettes and tea got to the point. "You've heard of Gen. Petraeus?" Lechner asked. Sattar said he had.

"He's heard of you too," Lechner told the sheik.

"He understands that you're the sheriff of this area. He'd like to ask you a very personal favor.

"He'd like you to recruit four hundred people into the army," Lechner said.

"No problem," Sattar said.

The next day, four hundred men walked through the gates of the compound where the recruiting drive was held.

Petraeus's first trip on assuming command in Iraq was to Anbar. The brigade and marine command staff crowded into the conference room at Camp Ramadi to brief the new general. The Ramadi numbers were compelling. They had gone from about a hundred police and two stations in May to more than three thousand police and government-sanctioned militia. There were functioning police stations throughout the city. The level of attacks had dropped to fourteen from twenty-two per day in the city. Insurgents had been attacking the government center as many as five times a day. Now, it was barely once a day. The key to it all was an alliance with tribal sheiks. Thousands of men who were once attacking Americans were now on their side. They had turned their guns on al-Qaeda.

"The key guy was Sheik Sattar and you'll want to meet him," MacFarland told Petraeus during the briefing.

Petraeus had come to Iraq knowing the importance of

reconciliation. As a division commander in Mosul in 2003 he was reaching out to low- and mid-level former Baathists, with permission of the U.S. administrator, Jerry Bremer. The Iraqi government would eventually put the brakes on those efforts, but he understood it was the only way these types of insurgencies could be defeated. He also was aware of several isolated efforts to reconcile with former insurgents and people straddling the fence. What was needed was "critical mass," an effort so powerful it would set off a chain reaction.

MacFarland was beginning to think Sattar might have a national role. Sattar had begun to make contacts with tribal leaders in other parts of the country. MacFarland thought if Petraeus and Sattar met it could help encourage other sheiks and regional leaders to support the Americans.

During the briefing, one of the officers suggested Sattar was only a minor sheik of an insignificant tribe. He went on to explain that Sattar ruled a minor tribe in the Dulaime federation and had a checkered past.

"I'm not worried about that," Petraeus said. "I want to meet him."

Petraeus had led an effort to overhaul the U.S. military's counterinsurgency doctrine and was personally involved in writing the new manual on irregular warfare. Understanding local dynamics and working through existing social structures is key to winning these kinds of wars. That means dealing with the world as it is rather than as you would like it to be. Ramadi was a perfect example of how to defeat an insurgency. "A blind man on a dark night could see we had some real potential and we needed to capitalize on it," Petraeus thought.

"This is nothing short of a miracle," Petraeus said.

"Why have I not heard this before?" Petraeus said, looking around the room. Someone offered weakly that the public affairs officer for the brigade had been killed.

Petraeus told MacFarland that he and his battalion commanders should get out more in front of the press.

"America needs war heroes."

Brig. Gen. John Allen, a scholarly marine officer and the deputy commander of the incoming marine headquarters, was responible for tribal relations, governance, "rule of law," and economic development. He had been following developments in Anbar closely, particularly the tribal revolt in Ramadi, as he prepared for his deployment. It was becoming clear that the tribes would be the key to pacifying Anbar. Allen, who had taught political science at the Naval Academy, was reading everything he could get his hands on about tribes. He studied Gertrude Bell, who had traveled along the Euphrates and lived among the tribes before becoming the oriental secretary to Sir Percy Cox, the British administrator in Mesopotamia after World War I.

The new command would need to figure out how to exploit the opening that the Awakening had provided. Reading Bell's observations gave Allen a sense of who the tribes are, what motivates them, and how they behave. The marines wanted to expand the tribal movement and also ensure that it was tied in to the government so it didn't represent a threat to the Shiite-backed government in Baghdad. They wanted to take it to the next level. Allen realized that Sattar and the Awakening, handled carefully, could help in Ramadi and in the larger effort.

"There was, I think, a sense in '06 that if you deal with this guy you're dealing with the devil and you're dealing with a criminal and how can we possibly do this," Allen said.

"The truth is, go find me someone in Anbar Province at that particular moment who wasn't smuggling. Go find me somebody who had never been involved in criminal activities. The answer was, there wasn't anybody."

The Awakening spread throughout Anbar in late 2006 and 2007, as more tribes allied themselves with the United States against al-Qaeda. The tougher problem was tying the tribes into the official provincial government in Anbar. Allen saw this as restoring a traditional role of having the sheiks lead while the politicians or technocrats govern. The provincial government, with the support of the marine command, agreed to expand the size of the council to seat members of the newly minted Awakening, while still reserving eleven seats for the more traditional sheiks.

About 30,000 surge troops began pouring into Iraq in spring 2007. Most went to Baghdad where they deployed in neighborhoods in much the way MacFarland placed outposts inside Ramadi a year earlier. By flooding the zone with U.S. troops and deploying them in neighborhoods, Petraeus slowed the violence. Tribes are not as influential in Baghdad, but the principle of providing local security, which worked in Ramadi, was applied in a slightly different way in Iraq's capital. The Americans began hiring small self-defense groups built around local or community leaders. Soon, tens of thousands of people in Baghdad were paid to provide security in their own neighborhoods. Many were former insurgents.

The next problem became bridging the gap between the Sunnis in Anbar and the Shiite-dominated government in Baghdad. The Sunnis had grown dependent on the Americans and viewed the central government with mistrust. Baghdad was slow to pay police and release government money for the province. Sattar's growing prominence helped. He spoke regularly with Prime Minister Nouri al-Maliki and helped build a relationship between the government and the Sunnis.

On January 17, 2007, MacFarland sat down to write condolence letters, which had been until recently a daily occurence. By the time the brigade left Iraq, eighty-three soldiers had been killed in Ramadi. The average age was twenty-four; every one was a volunteer.

On this day he would write to the family of Private First Class David Dietrich, twenty-one, who was killed a few days after Christmas. MacFarland had talked to Capt. Daniel Enslen, Dietrich's commander, to get some background on the soldier.

Dietrich came to the Brigade Reconnaissance Troop while the unit was already in Ramadi. Shortly before he moved up from Kuwait, the troop's first sergeant pulled aside Capt. Daniel Enslen, the commander of the BRT. "We've got an issue with this kid." The first sergeant had received some information on the new soldier when Dietrich was in Kuwait, preparing to head into Iraq. Dietrich had been to mental health counseling and appeared to have a learning disability. Enslen said they would make their own assessment when he arrived.

Enslen made a point of meeting all of the new replacements arriving in Iraq. The Brigade Reconnaissance Team was an elite unit of only about sixty-five soldiers, which was organized into small teams in Ramadi. Their main job was to kill insurgents planting roadside bombs. They had been doing that every day since they arrived in Ramadi in May and had one of the highest casualty rates of any unit in Ramadi. MacFarland had worried for a time that the unit's high casualty rates had left the troops with a sense of foreboding that would undermine their effectiveness. Enslen had assured MacFarland that they hadn't lost their edge. It was a tight group with high morale.

When Dietrich arrived in Iraq, Enslen was immediately impressed by the young soldier's enthusiasm and openness. Enslen was surprised that Dietrich talked so matter-of-factly about his boyhood. Dietrich's parents had abandoned him when he was a small boy and he lived with his grandfather until he was about fourteen and was kicked out of the house. After that he bounced around, staying with friends and families around Marysville, a tiny hamlet tucked into the hills of southern Pennsylvania. Sometimes he stayed at the Marysville Volunteer Fire Department and for a time lived in his white Chevrolet Blazer. Dinner was often microwave popcorn bought at a discount store. He was a slow learner. He struggled through boot camp and other soldiers had taken to calling him Forrest Gump.

When he arrived in Ramadi he came under the watchful eye of the first sergeant, a tough noncommissioned officer who kept a close eye on his troops. He constantly tested them on skills like clearing heavy machine guns and grenade launchers. If they couldn't conduct such procedures automatically and without thinking they were barred from the chow hall that day and had to make do with field rations.

Dietrich worked hard and routinely bugged his NCOs about being allowed outside the wire. He didn't join the army to sit on a big base. The first sergeant and others worked with Dietrich to teach him the soldiering skills needed to hit Ramadi's deadly streets. After about two months of training, the command thought he was ready. Dietrich was ecstatic.

His first mission was a patrol that was to set up countersniper positions in the northern part of the city where the marines were establishing a small combat outpost. His team set up a position in an upper floor of a building where they could observe the neighborhood. Dietrich had just taken his shift observing from the window. He noticed a man peering up at Dietrich's team and then disappearing. Dietrich drew closer to the window to get a better look.

A sniper's bullet passed through his Kevlar helmet and killed him instantly.

His team called for a medevac, but they couldn't get a vehicle near his position. Two of his teammates loaded his body on to a stretcher, running nearly half a mile while other members of the squad ran alongside and exchanged fire with insurgents.

Dietrich had made a mistake by approaching the window. It is better to stand back, remaining in the shadows, even if that limits visibility. The insurgent on the street may even have been there as bait, in an effort to draw out the Americans.

His comrades loaded his body on a helicopter for the start of its journey back to a town near the small village where he grew up.

The army had a tough time finding his parents to notify them of their son's death. Neither had phones. His mother was finally located in a shelter. The casualty officer got a voucher from the army so the mother could purchase a dress suitable for a funeral. His father found a clean shirt for the funeral, but his tennis shoes were filled with holes.

"We can all name stories about kids like David whose lives went very wrong," J. Craig Raisner, Dietrich's Scout leader, told the local newspaper.

"Something in him chose a different path."

MacFarland began to write.

20

Pure Blood

I drew these tides of men into my hands and wrote
my will across the sky in stars.

—T. E. LAWRENCE

A s the marine CH-46 helicopter banked and began its rat-
tling descent into Al Asad Air Base, Sheik Aifan Sadun al-
Issawi craned his neck to peer out the porthole into the
late-afternoon sun. Sadun was in his early thirties and had learned
English watching television. Sadun's eyes widened. There was no
mistaking the Boeing 747 with the distinctive blue markings sitting on the tarmac. Sadun and about ten other sheiks were given
a cover story: They were being brought to the U.S. base in Anbar
to meet with Petraeus and Ambassador Ray Crocker prior to their
testimony before Congress. Sadun now knew otherwise. Air
Force One was casting a long shadow across Iraq's western desert.
He turned to Brig. Gen. John Allen, who was seated across from
him, and broke out in a grin.

By September 2007 Anbar was an unmistakable success story, one that President Bush was anxious to highlight. He left the White House through a side door September 3, a Sunday evening, without the usual motorcade, and headed for Andrews Air Force Base. The plane departed after dark, with the shades drawn. Journalists who traveled with the president could tell only one editor about the secret trip and they couldn't use a cell phone to do it. It was Bush's third trip to Iraq since the war started, but he wasn't flying into Baghdad this time. He would land in the heart of Anbar Province. Bush's national security adviser, Stephen Hadley, told journalists on Air Force One that the turnaround in Anbar had been remarkable and Bush wanted to see it for himself. A presidential trip would also highlight success at a time when Bush's popularity was sinking amid a torrent of bad news from Iraq.

After a twelve-hour flight, Air Force One touched down at Al-Asad at 3:45 P.M. local time and taxied to a stop. The president was blasted with 115-degree heat when the door to Air Force One opened. "I had been told last summer that saving Anbar was impossible," Bush said at a short press conference. "That it was lost.

"Today, Anbar is a really different place."

He said he looked forward to meeting with the "tribal leaders who led the fight against the terrorists."

The marines had dispatched helicopters in several directions to pick up the sheiks, including Sadun, so they would get to Al-Asad in time for the meeting with Bush. They were led into a building on the air base where they would wait for the president, who was visiting troops on another part of the base. Secret service agents were set up to screen the visitors. Allen went first, relinquishing his M4 carbine and 9mm pistol to the agents. As a military officer he wasn't required to surrender his weapon, but he wanted to show the sheiks that it was something everyone had to do. Trust was important to them.

As the sheiks waited anxiously in the air-conditioned anteroom, Allen took Gov. Mamoun Sami Rashid al-Alwani aside and brought him inside the room where the sheiks and provincial leaders would meet the president. Place cards were set around the table. Allen was concerned about the priority of seating for the sheiks. Among themselves, sheiks quickly sort themselves in order of seniority. They were sensitive to rank. Having closely studied the tribes, Allen sought to arrange the seating so that the senior sheik sat next to the president.

"I've done the best I can to lay out the seniority of the sheiks here," Allen told Mamoun, showing him the table.

Sattar was growing in prominence, but was still a junior sheik of a minor tribe. Allen had placed Sattar near the end of the table, at one of the seats farthest from where the president would sit.

Mamoun looked at the place cards, picked up Sattar's, and put it right next to the president.

Allen was surprised. Sattar and Mamoun had been at odds for at least a year. Mamoun had viewed Sattar as a threat.

"Well, you know, he is a pretty junior guy," Allen said.

"He should sit next to the president," Mamoun said.

Mamoun had come to understand there was no point in resisting Sattar's growing power. Better to align himself with the

sheik. It was a measure of how the political dynamics of Anbar—
and the country—had changed. Sattar had risen from a minor
sheik and smuggler to a power broker in a year. Now he was not
only about to meet the president of the United States, but would
do so as the province's most prominent sheik and the man who
helped defeat al-Qaeda in western Iraq.

Bush finished visiting with the troops and entered the room,
greeting the Iraqis, which included security officials, government leaders, and tribal sheiks. The president took his place on
one side of the long table. He was flanked by Gov. Mamoun
on his right and Sattar on his left. President Jalal Talabani and
Prime Minister Nouri al-Maliki sat across the table from Bush.

As the governor, Mamoun spoke first. He launched into
complaints about the central government in Baghdad, aiming his
remarks across the table at al-Maliki. He said Baghdad ignored
Anbar and withheld money from the Sunni province. There was
an uncomfortable silence when he finished. Al-Maliki, glaring
across the table at Mamoun, was not happy. The U.S. officials
seated behind Bush were quietly seething. They were holding a
reconstruction conference in Anbar in a few days and Baghdad's
cooperation was critical. Humiliating al-Maliki in front of the
president of the United States was not a good idea.

Bush broke the silence. "When I was a governor in Texas, I
had the same feelings about Washington." The room erupted in
laughter.

The marines had made it clear that Sattar would be the one
to address the president when it came time for the tribal leaders
to speak. Sattar, though he had little time to prepare his remarks,

instinctively knew what to say. He fixed the president in his gaze and through an interpreter launched into a short speech.

"Mr. President, please tell the American people that we appreciate the sacrifices of their sons and daughters. And that their losses, the losses of their parents, are our losses as well, and we feel and grieve for the death of the coalition brothers and sisters just as we grieve for the members of our tribe."

He went on to talk about his vision for Anbar and his hopes that the government in Baghdad would represent all Iraqis. Sattar was careful to speak for all the tribes. Their leaders nodded their heads in approval as he spoke.

Bush listened and on a couple of occasions pulled out a piece of paper from his jacket and jotted notes. He appeared moved. Here was a fighter; someone who could be counted on.

"Mr. President, when we are done in Anbar Province we will come with you and fight the Taliban in Afghanistan."

Bush was charmed. "I wish I could get help like this in Afghanistan from everybody," the president said, in apparent reference to the reluctance of NATO allies to send troops.

Lt. Col. Miciotto Johnson, whose battalion replaced Deane's unit when it rotated out of Iraq, had struck up a close relationship with Sattar. Johnson spent part of nearly every day at Sattar's compound.

The two had lunch at Sattar's home several days after the meeting with Bush. It wasn't the usual massive spread. Sattar called it a traditional poor man's meal. It was chicken and soup.

"We sat there at the dining-room table, just joking," Johnson said.

Sattar wouldn't stop talking about his meeting with Bush. "That was his ultimate dream," Johnson said.

Johnson tried to change the subject. "Sattar, you have to be very careful now. You can't go out of this compound without your up-armor [armored vehicles]." Sattar's brother Ahmad had purchased two armored Land Cruisers.

Sattar's face was known throughout the Arab world, largely due to his media strategy and his growing prominence in Iraq. He had openly challenged al-Qaeda and his lucrative relationship with the United States had made other tribes jealous. He was a marked man.

Johnson had brought along Matt Sanchez, a journalist and marine reservist who had reported extensively from Iraq. Sattar was still pumped up from his meeting with Bush and was particularly animated. He entered the room in his formal tribal dress, unfastening his holster with a flourish and handing his revolver to a beefy bodyguard so he could sit down. The pistol reminded Sanchez of the cannon-sized handgun that Clint Eastwood carried in *Dirty Harry*. Sattar explained that it was important that a weapon be not only deadly but also impressive looking.

Sattar took Sanchez out to show him his falcons. Hunting with the birds is a Bedouin tradition dating back centuries. An aide held one of the fearsome-looking birds as Sattar launched into a short lecture on the beauty of birds of prey. It was difficult to say whether Sattar was pandering to the popular notion of tribal sheiks in the American mind or whether he really believed

it. Perhaps he had come to believe in the myth he had so carefully created.

Sattar told Sanchez about his meeting with the president
and said it was too bad Bush was losing popularity in America.
He said he admired Bush for sticking to his principles despite
public opinion. He spoke of his fathers and brothers who were
killed by al-Qaeda and boasted of his role in starting the Awakening and standing up to terrorists.

"I'm the only one who stood in their face."

He also talked about Travis Patriquin, saying he was a great
patriot and that his death affected him.

"Throughout Iraqi history, September has always been a
month of momentous change," Sattar told Sanchez.

"It is also the month of my birth. I hope these two events
will have significance."

Tribes are constantly jockeying for power and status, but no one
leader can stick his neck out too far. Sattar seemed reckless in
his disregard for the conventions. It's what got him as far as he
had. He wasn't about to change his style.

Johnson was worried about Sattar. On June 30, the commander's men stumbled on to an insurgent meeting and ended
up in a vicious all-night firefight against about forty to sixty militants. Two Americans and dozens of insurgents were killed in the
fighting. Intelligence gathered after the battle, which was fought
south of Ramadi near a place called Donkey Island, suggested
insurgents were making careful plans to assassinate Sattar and

launch attacks into parts of Ramadi under the Awakening's influence. The Americans had found a video with militants denouncing Sattar. A classified assessment in July concluded that al-Qaeda was building up forces in the Ramadi area, probably in anticipation of an attack on Sattar and his tribal allies. The fighters were well trained and armed. "They could have caused enough of a commotion and chaos as to put significant doubt in the minds of the residents regarding the wisdom of their rejection of AQI [al-Qaeda in Iraq]," according to a secret intelligence report. In other words, a big enough attack could have killed the Awakening as it was gathering momentum.

The army got lucky. The lopsided U.S. victory at Donkey Island probably aborted a major effort to kill Sattar. The Americans, however, knew there were plenty of other threats out there.

Sattar's compound had been attacked with car bombs twice in October 2006. In July 2007 a suicide bomber accidentally drove his truck into a ditch. Intelligence officers thought the target might have been Sattar's home.

Throughout the summer of 2007 intelligence about al-Qaeda intentions in Anbar was flooding into the U.S. military. Al-Qaeda wanted to "shatter the image that is being portrayed in Western and pan-Arab media of Ramadi being a model city," according to a secret report.

"The loss of the Euphrates River valley is a huge loss to them," Gen. David Petraeus said of al-Qaeda. "They have to try and respond."

It wasn't just al-Qaeda that was gunning for Sattar. "Once you attain power you're going to have challenges and they are

going to come after you," said William McCallister, the retired
army officer who was a tribal adviser to the marine command.

"The chances of someone getting whacked are always good."

Sattar had climbed into his unarmored Land Cruiser on September 13, the first day of Ramadan, to check on his horses. The
stables were outside the secured perimeter of Sattar's compound,
but within his property.

Johnson was out with his security detail, checking on police
stations at about 3 P.M. when he heard the explosion. At Camp
Ramadi, Capt. David Bradley saw a huge plume of smoke coming from Sattar's compound and scrambled to the roof of a nearby
building to get a better look. Johnson sent a patrol to Sattar's
compound to investigate.

They quickly reported back, addressing the commander directly.

"Tiger six, you need to come over."

It was chaos. Men and women were screaming and crying.

"What's going on!" Johnson yelled as he climbed out of his
Humvee.

"They got Sattar."

A group of men were carrying the tribal leader's limp body
carefully into his home. The unarmored SUV was a twisted, smoking wreckage. The attackers left nothing to chance. They had
packed sixty to eighty pounds of homemade explosive into the
roadside bomb and detonated it as Sattar crossed a small canal
about 140 yards northwest of his house. It appeared to have been
triggered by remote control, as a circuit board had been discov-

ered at the scene. Sattar and two bodyguards were killed instantly. His SUV was torn open by the blast.

In the end it was probably a mixture of tribal rivalry and al-Qaeda that led to Sattar's death. One of his guards had been bribed to let the attackers close enough to set up the bomb. Sattar had been in a fight with a tribe located south of Lake Habaniyah. The tribe had been smuggling oil and sharing revenue with al-Qaeda—either out of intimidation or because they were allied with the militants. Either way, Sattar warned the sheik to stop. Smuggling oil was okay, but no revenues were to go to al-Qaeda. When the tribal leader didn't get the message, his trucks were shot up. When he confronted Sattar, he was publicly dismissed.

"Then it became an honor issue," Allen said.

Petraeus was in the United States, having just finished testimony before Congress on the status of the Iraq War. He had given the lawmakers a cautious assessment. The new "surge" strategy was working, but the gains were reversible. Petraeus was excruciatingly careful in his description of developments in Iraq to stick to the evidence and avoid sweeping judgments or any happy talk.

He needed to navigate a very fine line. He was returning to Washington near the height of a heated presidential debate at the center of which was the Iraq War. He was greeted in Washington with a newspaper advertisement headlined GENERAL BETRAY US from the liberal group Moveon.org. He faced questioning from Senators McCain, Hillary Clinton, and Barack Obama, all of whom were running for president and were anxious to stake out a position on Iraq. There was still a lot of skepticism among the Democrats.

"The reports that you provide to us really require the willing suspension of disbelief," Clinton told Petraeus and Ambassador Ray Crocker.

The day after his testimony, Petraeus was sitting down with a group of editors at *The Washington Post* when an aide, Col. Steve Boylan, passed him a note. Sattar had been killed.

Allen was on his third day of leave, home briefly from Iraq, and was lifting weights at a gym at Camp Lejeune. His wife rushed into the room, visibly shaken. "Call Anbar right now."

In Baghdad, the insurgents were ecstatic. The bond of Americans and tribal leaders in Ramadi was the most formidable opponent al-Qaeda had faced in Iraq. Insurgent leaders were spreading the word, saying it was now safe to return to Ramadi, al-Qaeda's former capital in Iraq.

Later that day at the Pentagon, Petraeus acknowledged the assassination was a "tragic loss." But he went on to say that he didn't think it would undermine the Awakening and the momentum it had started.

A classified intelligence report from the marine command backed up the general's assessment. Sattar's assassination "is not likely to deter the forward progress of anti-AQI movements in al-Anbar," the report said. The movement had too much support. The death of one man wouldn't derail it.

Within days of the killing, another classified report noted encouraging signs. "The martyrdom of Sheik Sattar did not prove to be the blow that AQI likely anticipated and instead may have made the [Awakening] movement even stronger and renewed the resolve of the people of al-Anbar," the intelligence report concluded.

"Although they killed Sattar, there are a million Sattars in

Anbar," Sattar's brother, Ahmad, declared when he assumed the leadership of the organization. Ahmad lacked the charisma of Sattar, but he was better suited to turn the Awakening into a political movement. He was a steadier hand, less volatile than his younger brother.

U.S. military dignitaries and Iraqi politicians packed Sattar's funeral. Prime Minister Nouri al-Maliki and President Jalal Talabani released statements. Talabani compared him to the major heroes of Iraq's past. "The best way to avenge the blood of heroes, like immortal Sheik Abu Risha, is through insistence on continuing to move along the path of the glorious struggle and jihad, which is lit by their pure blood."

It is hard to imagine that Sattar, who knew better than most the dangers of taking on al-Qaeda and upsetting the natural balance of tribes, thought he would live to see the Awakening flower into a national movement.

"He knew that he wasn't going to survive this," McAllister said.

After his brigade left Iraq, MacFarland moved to the Pentagon, where he was assigned to the Joint Chiefs of Staff. In October 2007 he flew to Iraq as part of a small group of staff officers led by Marine Lt. Gen. John Sattler. The team flew to Fallujah for briefings and on to Ramadi, meeting up with commanders in Anbar. During a private moment, Marine Brig. Gen. John Allen told MacFarland that the city's transformation would not have been possible without the work of his brigade and MacFarland's personal cultivation of Sattar.

Ever the armor officer, MacFarland had thought of his brigade as a breaching force. The next wave of forces would pour through the opening, solidifying gains while pursuing the enemy. The breaching force carries the battle from defeat to victory across a line that is only visible in retrospect. It is easy to forget how a rapid advance began once it is under way, MacFarland thought. We tend to become mesmerized by the progress of the exploitation.

The convoy drove down Route Michigan, through the heart of the city. A year earlier, American vehicles would have been fighting their way from one end of the city to the other. MacFarland noticed that posters with pictures of Sattar and Lt. Col. Salaam abu Alwani—the officer who tracked the killers of Patriquin—were plastered along the streets. Salaam was killed by a car bomb in February 2007. Both men were celebrated on the posters as martyrs.

The convoy turned on to Seventeenth Street and stopped at the first bend in the road. They got out, removing their body armor and helmets. A growing throng of curious children accompanied the Americans as they walked toward Checkpoint 296, at the edge of downtown. MacFarland made mental notes of places where he had survived roadside bomb blasts and rocket-propelled grenade attacks. They passed the area where al-Qaeda had staged a parade for the international media. They strolled by the old Saddam Mosque, now called the Awakening Mosque. A police station had been named after Patriquin. The streets were alive with motorcycles, taxis, pedestrians, and construction vehicles. Concrete blast walls and concertina wires had been removed and the blackened potholes caused by IEDs had been repaired. What barriers remained had been painted with bright colors and patterns.

MacFarland thought of the hundreds of Americans who had died and the thousands who had been injured fighting on these streets. Their families would never see the city as he had.

At Checkpoint 296, once the gateway into one of the world's most violent cities, the officers climbed back into their vehicles and drove down Route Michigan toward the government center. The rubble in the surrounding blocks had been cleared and the building itself had been repaired. Blast walls and concertina wire had been removed and the government center was now open to the street. Inside was a functioning government.

It was still Ramadan, only three weeks since Sattar had been killed. As sundown approached, shops and restaurants began lifting their shutters to sell warm flatbread for the evening meal, when Muslims would break their daily fast. Kebab vendors fanned the coals beneath their grills, sending showers of sparks into the darkening sky.

NOTES

The bulk of the research for this book is based on about a hundred interviews with participants in the battle for Ramadi in 2006. Many of the officers and soldiers remain on active duty and are scattered around the world. I conducted the interviews in Iraq, Afghanistan, and Washington, D.C. Nearly every subject agreed to speak on the record. I have also relied on thousands of pages of documents, including declassified Marine Corps intelligence reports, interviews conducted by the U.S. Marine Corps History Division and the U.S. Army Combat Studies Institute, various miltary reports, and journal articles. I have also had access to contemporary notes, journals, and e-mails from many participants in the 2006 Ramadi campaign.

Throughout the book I have used the ranks of individuals current in 2006. I have updated the rank and job status of some of the people in Where They Are Now.

In the case of Arabic names and words I have attempted to settle on the most common English transliterations. On subsequent reference of names, I have used the Arabic convention of using the first name.

1: Hero Flight

The doors opened: The account of the hero flight was based on author interviews with Lt. Col. Tony Deane, First Sgt. David Shaw, Col. Sean MacFarland, Chaplain Michael Wood, and Sgt. Jesus Cadena.

Tribble was raised: The account of Tribble's upbringing was based on author interviews with his mother, Tracy Tribble, and his army buddy, Jason Dickerson.

Tribble had been in Iraq: The details of the patrol was based on author interviews with Dickerson and Sgt. Tom Davis.

2: Sideshow

At 7 A.M., May 22: The description of the first day was based on author interviews with Col. Sean MacFarland.

Even inside the small compound: Description of Ramadi's government center was based on personal observation.

He had survived: Jim Michaels, *USA Today*, November 7, 2007.

The new president elected: A news account and transcript of the speech appeared in *The New York Times*, May 28, 1981.

MacFarland was the son and grandson: Upbringing and family background was based on author interviews with MacFarland.

MacFarland was introverted: The account of MacFarland's junior officer days was based on author interviews with him and J. W. Thurman.

Operation Bridge Builder: MacFarland interview with Combat Studies Institute, January 17, 2008.

"Who sent this guy here?" Gates thought: Author interview with Teddy Gates, May 18, 2009.

"Al Anbar is going to be": Marine Lt. Gen. John F. Sattler in *The New York Times*, June 26, 2006.

3: Valley of the Gun

The man stared: The account of this fight was based on an interview with Sgt. Jesus Cadena and army documents supporting his nomination for a Bronze Star medal.

"You own that street": Author interview with Maj. Eric Remoy, First Brigade, First Armored Division intelligence officer, November 10, 2008.

In April, Sterling Jensen: Journal kept by Sterling Jensen.

4: Back to the Brawl

Epigraph: Maj. Gen. James Mattis, commander of the First Marine Division, interview, U.S.M.C. History Division, June 17, 2009. Cited in T. S. McWilliams and K. P. Wheeler, eds., *Al-Anbar Awakening*, vol. 1: *American Perspectives* (Quantico, Va.: Marine Corps University Press, 2009); hereafter, U.S.M.C. History Division.

"We are going back into the brawl": "A Letter to All Hands" from Mattis, March 23, 2004.

For this kind of "war": Mattis, U.S.M.C. History Division interview.

The Pentagon liked metrics: Mattis, U.S.M.C. History Division interview.

"What matters most": Mattis, U.S.M.C. History Division interview.

"Tribes would be the center": Mattis, U.S.M.C. History Division interview.

Mattis was traveling: Mattis, U.S.M.C. History Division interview.

"Who sent them into Fallujah": Lt. Gen. James Conway, commander First Marine Expeditionary Force, interview, U.S.M.C. History Division, June 21 and July 7, 2005.

"Okay, just continue": Mattis, U.S.M.C. History Division interview.

"Four white guys in a soft-skinned vehicle": Conway, U.S.M.C. History Division interview.

"I don't want to go into the city": Mattis, U.S.M.C. History Division interview.

"Once we had Fallujah": Conway, U.S.M.C. History Division interview.

President Bush was among: Bing West, *No True Glory, A Frontline Account of the Battle for Fallujah* (New York: Bantam Books, 2005).

Conway argued with his: Conway, U.S.M.C. History Division interview.

"I asked that we": Mattis, U.S.M.C. History Division interview.

"We're trying to stick": Mattis, U.S.M.C. History Division interview.

"We've got fifty guys": Conway, U.S.M.C. History Division interview.

"It taught us": Conway, U.S.M.C. History Division interview.

"We can give you the city": Conway, U.S.M.C. History Division interview.

They could "go out": Maj. Gen. Richard F. Natonski, commander of First Marine Division, interview, U.S.M.C. History Division, March 16, 2005.

"The second worst thing": Author interview with Marine Maj. Ben Connable, September 20, 2009.

The night before: Lt. Gen. John Sattler, commander of First Marine Expeditionary Force, interview, U.S.M.C. History Division, April 8, 2005.

Some were high on: Sattler, U.S.M.C. History Division interview.

"Fallujah changed the balance": Author interview with Connable.

"We made Fallujah": Author interview with Connable.

Even as Marines: Bing West, *No True Glory*.

"All we found": Conway, U.S.M.C. History Division interview.

"We knew Fallujah": Author interview with Connable.

5: Fix Ramadi

Epigraph: J.F.C. Fuller, *The Generalship of Alexander the Great* (London: Eyre & Spottiswoode, 1958).

"We had all heard the stories": Author interview with MacFarland, April 28, 2008.

"Our focus coming out here": Maj. Gen. Richard C. Zilmer, commander of First Marine Expeditionary Force (forward), interview, U.S.M.C. History Division, January 1, 2007.

"We understood that despite": Author interview with Connable.

They developed a plan: Author interview with Connable.

"That was a blatant lie": Connable, interview, U.S.M.C. History Division, June 26, 2009. Connable was a foreign area officer on the First Marine Expeditionary Force staff in 2003 and 2004. In 2005 and 2006 he served as an intelligence analyst for both the First and Second Marine Expeditionary Forces.

"These guys just didn't get": Author interview with Connable.

"Fix Ramadi": Col. Sean MacFarland, interview by Steven E. Clay, January 17, 2008, Fort Leavenworth, Kans., Combat Studies Institute.

"I wasn't really quite sure": MacFarland interview, Combat Studies Institute.

"They were treading water": Author interview with Lt. Col. Pete Lee, August 1, 2009.

"We were building the brigade": Author interview with Col. John Gronski, September 16, 2009.

"The more we'd fight, the more": Author interview with Marine Maj. Teddy Gates, May 18, 2009.

They lost eighty-two soldiers: Author interview with Gronski.

"These are Pennsylanvia coal miners": Author interview with Col. Pete Devlin, December 2, 2008.

"I made a conscious decision": Author interview with Gronski.

"The fault lies with whoever sent Two-Twenty-eight": Author interview with Lt. Col. Jim Lechner, November 20, 2008.

"What was that?": Author interview with Lt. Col. Ron Clark, May 14, 2009.

Zilmer told MacFarland: Author interview with MacFarland.

"You never know where a sniper round": Author interview with MacFarland.

"We hear they're going to clear it like": Author interviews with Clark and Remoy.

"They basically vacated their strongholds": Author interview with Clark.

"They thought we were": Author interview with Remoy.

"Sooner or later they will": Author interview with MacFarland.

6: Falcon

"You guys are going": Author interview with Sterling Jensen, February 11, 2009; and in Thomas E. Ricks, *The Gamble: General David Petreaus and the American Military Adventure in Iraq, 2006–2008* (New York: The Penguin Press, 2009).

"If you go in there you're": Author interview with Capt. Mike Bajema, September 14, 2009.

The heavy tanks and armored vehicles: Author interview with Connable.

"That completely pulled the shroud": Author interview with Lt. Col. V. J. Tedesco, May 26, 2009.

His battalion ended up firing about a hundred main: Author interview with Tedesco.

The battalion lost twenty-five tanks: Jim Michaels, "An Army Colonel's Gamble Pays Off," *USA Today*, May 1, 2007.

They gave each of seven families: Author interview with Bajema.

For the next three days: Author interview with Bajema.

Tedesco told Bajema: Author interview with Bajema.

Bajema's company was aggressive: Author interview with Bajema.

It didn't get any better: Author interview with Bajema.

Once at Falcon: Author interview with Bajema.

In less than two weeks: Author interview with MacFarland.

"We knew what block they were on": Author interview with Bajema.

A sniper round hit: Bajema author interview; Dick Couch, *The Sheriff of Ramadi: Navy SEALs and the Winning of al-Anbar* (Annapolis, Maryland: Naval Institute Press, 2008).

There were probably fifty: Author interview with Bajema.

"Mike, what's going on?": Author interview with Bajema.

The SEALs, meanwhile: Dick Couch, *The Sheriff of Ramadi;* author interview with Bajema.

The SEALs managed to kill: Author interview with Bajema.

They had used more than: Author interview with Bajema. The description of the attack on the government center and establishing an outpost near the racetrack was based on author interviews with Capt. Jayson Arthaud on February 18, 2009, and Lt. Col. Bill Jurney on December 16, 2008.

7: Counterattack

Epigraph: From an interview conducted by the Marine Corps History Division in G. W. Montgomery and T. S. McWilliams, eds., *Al-Anbar Awakening,* vol. 2: *Iraqi Perspectives* (Quantico, Va.: Marine Corps University Press, 2009). The subject is the wife of a police officer in Ramadi. She was identified only by a pseudonym.

Lechner's small convoy: The description of the attack that killed Capt. Jason West was based on author interviews with Lt. Col. Jim Lechner and Sterling Jensen and on Jensen's journal, cited in chapter 3.

Lechner, a former Ranger: Lechner's experience in Somalia is described in Mark Bowden's *Black Hawk Down: A Story of Modern War* (New York: Penguin Books, 1999).

"We have lost a guy": Jensen's journal.

The ambush on Route Michigan: Brigade After Action report.

The brigade had received intelligence reports: Author interview with Remoy.

But Marine Maj. Gen. Richard Zilmer: Author interview with MacFarland.

"I just wanted a pulse check": Author interview with Maj. Michael Wood, the brigade chaplain, February 4, 2009.

MacFarland recounted to his staff: Author interview with MacFarland.

8: Sheik Sattar

"We thought he had a death wish": Author interview with Capt. Sean Frerking, November 17, 2008.

First Sgt. Robin Bolmer spent many late nights: Author interview with First. Sgt. Robin Bolmer, April 22, 2009.

"I'm going to paraphrase L.B.J.": Author interview with Lt. Col. Tony Deane, May 8, 2008.

"It takes consensus to create a sheik": Author interview with William "Mac" McCallister, a tribal adviser to the marine headquarters in Anbar; McCallister was profiled in an excellent article by Greg Jaffe in *The Wall Street Journal,* September 10, 2007.

Throughout history: For background and history on tribes in Iraq I relied on several books, including *Tribes and Power: Nationalism and Ethnicity in the Middle East,* edited by Faleh A. Jabar and Hosham Dawod; Phebe Marr's *The Modern History of Iraq*; and Hanna Batatu's *The Old Social Classes and the Revolutionary Movements of Iraq.*

Gen. David Petraeus, who would assume: Author interview with Gen. David Petraeus, December 4, 2009.

What set Sattar apart from most other sheiks: Author interview with Devlin.

"I was always against these terrorists": Quoted in Todd Pittman, Associated Press, March 25, 2007.

Sattar's father, Bezia Ftekhan al-Rishawi: Brigade Bilat report, December 4, 2006.

After attending a funeral in 2005: Interview with Ahmad Abu Risha conducted by Zaid Sabah, an Iraqi journalist. A Multi-National Corps-Iraq declassified intelligence report said Sattar's father was killed in November 2004.

Three of Sattar's brothers were killed: Ahmad Abu Risha interview by Zaid Sabah.

9: Awakening

They were directed to: The account of the initial Awakening meeting is based primarily on a description provided by Deane during several interviews.

This was not the first time: The account of the Anbar People's Committee, a failed earlier tribal revolt against al-Qaeda, is based primarily on author interviews with Connable, MacFarland, and Marine Lt. Gen. John Allen. Some of the details also came from Marine Corps History Division interviews with Connable, and Marine Maj. Lester Gerber, the intelligence officer for Third Battalion, Eighth Marines when they were in Ramadi. Recollections of the numbers of sheiks who were killed during the failed revolt vary. Gerber said seven of the nine original principals were assassinated during a two-week period in late 2005. A declassified intelligence report said eight of the organizers were assassinated.

Americans would stay on their bases and local: Marine Corps History Division interview with Gerber.

The marines had received a report: Author interview with Connable.

Provincewide attack levels around that time: Author interview with Connable and U.S.M.C. History Division interview with Connable.

On election day: U.S.M.C. History Division interview with Gerber.

"Instead of that, General George Casey": U.S.M.C. History Division interview with Connable and author interview with Connable.

"We've reached a turning point here": Author interview with Col. John Gronski, commander of the Second Brigade, Twenty-eighth Infantry, Pennsylvania National Guard, September 16, 2009.

They put together a hit list of about: Author interview with Connable.

Sattar had wanted no part: There are conflicting reports about whether Sattar was part of the Anbar People's Committee. The brigade Bilat report of December 3 suggests he was at least nominally a member. Even if he was part of the committee, he viewed most members as rivals and was likely harboring his own ambitions.

He also believed it was a mistake: Brigade Bilat report, December 3, 2006.

10: "This Is Iraq"

Epigraph: MacFarland interview by Clay, January 17, 2008.

About twenty sheiks: Details of the September 9, 2006, meeting were compiled from author interviews with MacFarland, Deane, Jensen, and notes taken by Jensen at the meeting.

"He put himself in a position": Author interview with Capt. Matt Alden, April 27, 2009.

"If this goes wrong, we are all dead": Author interview with Capt. Pat Fagan, February 2, 2009.

Marine Lt. Col. Kris Stillings was attempting: Author interview with Stillings, February 10, 2009.

Gates knew that al-Qaeda would attempt: Details of the bombing of the Jazeera police station were provided by author interviews with Teddy Gates, MacFarland, Jensen, and Marine Staff Sgt. Eric Baker, who provided an e-mail account of what he witnessed.

"We have felt like men": Jensen journal.

"He'll never come back": Jensen journal.

"Soon there were no men left to kill": Interview with unnamed woman in *Al-Anbar Awakening*, vol. 2: *Iraqi Perspectives*.

During Ramadan in 2005: Interview with unnamed woman in *Al-Anbar Awakening*, vol. 2: *Iraqi Perspectives*.

"They would behead a person": Interview with Maj. Gen. Tariq Yusif Mohammad al-Thiyabi in *Al-Anbar Awakening*, vol. 2: *Iraqi Perspectives*.

Once, when al-Qaeda militants stopped: Interview with Sheik Ali Hatim Abd al-Razzaq Ali Al-Sulayman al-Assafi in *Al-Anbar Awakening*, vol. 2: *Iraqi Perspectives*.

"Leave it to me": Interview with Sheik Ahmad al-Rishawi in *Al-Anbar Awakening*, vol. 2: *Iraqi Perspectives*.

He called Sheik Wissam: Sheik Wissam Abd al-Ibrahim in *Al-Anbar Awakening*, vol. 2: *Iraqi Perspectives*.

11: Secret Talks

Epigraph: Al-Issawi was quoted in the Marine Corps History Division, *Al-Anbar Awakening*, vol. 2: *Iraqi Perspectives*.

Brig. Gen. David Reist had: Author interview with Reist, deputy commanding general of First Marine Expeditionary Force, February 20, 2009.

An anti-American imam was giving a fiery: Author interview with Jerry Jones, a special assistant to Defense Secretary Donald Rumsfeld, April 16, 2009.

The Texas businessman who had e-mailed Reist: Author interview with Ken Wischkaemper, March 11, 2009.

They had played a role: Iraq Survey Group final report, September 30, 2004.

"All of a sudden I realized these guys": Author interview with Marine Col. Mike Walker, April 22, 2009.

"He was afraid for his safety": Author interview with Lt. Col. Dave Harlan, April 21, 2009.

He talked about the treatment: Notes from the meeting dated July 19, 2004.

The messenger then asked: Meeting notes.

Army Gen. George Casey, then top U.S. commander in Iraq, called: August 30, 2004, e-mail message from Casey to Maj. Gen. Henry Stratman, chief of staff for political and economic affairs, Multi-National Forces–Iraq.

He ordered Jones to "cease and desist": David Rose wrote about these Amman negotiations in *Vanity Fair*, in an online-only article, http://www.vanityfair.com/politics/features/2009/05/iraqi-insurgents200905. Wolfowitz told Rose that he wasn't opposed to reaching out to Sunnis but "it had to the done through the appropriate channels, not by free-lancing through the secretary of defense's office."

12: Angel on the Shoulder

Epigraph: *The Old Social Classes and the Revolutionary Movements of Iraq.*

Sattar reclined in front: Scene described in author interview with Alden.

"He's close to me": Author interview with Jensen.

One of Sattar's bodyguards: Bilat report, December 2, 2006.

"TAA doesn't exist": Bilat report, December 2, 2006.

On October 25, 2006: Brigade PowerPoint slide.

"Tell your friends who put up": Jensen journal.

When the Americans needed extra danger pay: Several American officers and a document confirmed the CIA assistance in providing the extra police pay.

At his house one day: Bilat report, December 2, 2006.

13: Sympathy for the Devil

Epigraph: Author interview with Devlin.

"First, burn or capture all the boats": Bilat report, December 3, 2006.

"The guy's a criminal": Author interview with Deane.

They were making a fortune: Author interview with Devlin.

A secret message based on reporting: Beyond oil smuggling, allegations surrounding Sattar are vague.

As late as March 2007: Tribal Leader Biography, declassified Multi-National Corps–Iraq report dated March 15, 2007.

American interrogators were puzzled: Tribal Leader Biography, March 15, 2007.

"Even if only 2 percent was true": Interview with Sheik Abdul Rahman in *Al-Anbar Awakening*, vol. 2: *Iraqi Perspectives.*

The Sunni populace in Anbar: Author interview with James Soriano, Provincial Reconstruction team leader in Anbar Province, May 14, 2009.

"Clerics who preach politics are frauds": Author interview with Soriano.

The British chose Ramadi: Gertrude Bell describes the scene in a letter dated July 31, 1921; details are also from Georgina Howell's *Gertrude Bell: Queen of the Desert, Shaper of Nations* (New York: Farrar, Straus and Giroux, 2006).

But he was implicated in the killing: Peter Sluglett's *Britain in Iraq: Contriving King and Country* (London: I.B. Tauris & Co., Ltd., 2007).

Yet the generals could scarcely be expected: Lt. Gen. Aylmer L. Haldane, who commanded British forces in Iraq after World War I, wrote about his experience in *The Insurrection in Mesopotamia 1920* (London: Imperial War Museum, Department of Printed Books, 2005).

Even "the paramount Shaikh depend": British administrative reports.

Saddam excelled at: Accounts of the rebellion appeared in *The New York Times* and *The Times* in the U.K.

The city was sealed off: BBC report.

They began hijacking and looting trucks: BBC report.

Lt. Gen. Graeme Lamb, a British officer: Author interview with Jensen.

"He was a regular scallywag": Author interview with Lt. Gen. Graeme Lamb, September 15, 2009.

14: The Chairman's Briefing

Marine Gen. Peter Pace . . . looked almost ashen: The account of the meeting is based on the recollections of Devlin in author interview with Devlin.

Weeks later a story about the memo: Thomas E. Ricks, "Situation Called Dire in West Iraq; Anbar Is Lost Politically, Marine Analyst Says," *The Washington Post*, September 11, 2006, p. 1.

"It made me mad": Author interview with Teddy Gates.

"I had a lot of flexibility": Jim Michaels, "An Army Colonel's Gamble Pays Off," *USA Today*, May 1, 2007.

15: Shark Fin

Epigraph: Reports of Administration for 1918, quoted in Batatu.

The call came on: The account of the Shark Fin battle comes principally from author interviews with Lt. Col. Chuck Ferry, Lechner, Jensen, and Col. Gary Montgomery of the Marine Corps History Division. I also relied on Montgomery's interview with Sheik Jassim Muhammad Saleh al-Suwadawi in *Al-Anbar Awakening*, vol. 2: *Iraqi Perspectives*, and PowerPoint slides produced by Montgomery that show the outline of the battle. Jassim claimed that his tribe was attacked by 850 al-Qaeda militants and they killed more than 90 of them. U.S. officers consider that estimate to be unreliable.

He had sold his last cow: Sheik Jassim quoted in *Al-Anbar Awakening*, vol. 2: *Iraqi Perspectives*.

Sattar's alliance was able: Sheik Wissam interview in *Al-Anbar Awakening*, vol. 2: *Iraqi Perspectives*.

The sheik returned to his tribal area: Author interview with Lechner and MacFarland interview with the Center for Army Lessons Learned.

Abu Ayoub al-Masri: Author interviews with Remoy and Lechner.

Within hours, Lechner and Patriquin: Author interview with Lechner.

"Who are these guys?": Author interview with Lechner.

The decision to jump into: Author interview with Capt. Niel Smith, November 6, 2008.

16: Wisam

Epigraph: Joyce was quoted in an article in the October 2003 issue of *Military History* magazine by O'Brien Browne.

Sattar was outside his house: The description of the scene at Sattar's home a week after the Shark Fin battle was described in the brigade Bilat report dated December 2, 2006.

"It looked like": Author interview with Marine Col. Steve Zotti, November 14, 2008.

On one operation: Declassified intelligence report on Sattar.

"You are the mujahedeen": Author interview with navy chaplain, Commander Dennis Rocheford, a navy chaplain, February 20, 2009.

Before the Ready First left: Author interview with Capt. Russ Wagner, July 31, 2009.

"Hey, guys, you're not going to believe this": Author interview with Wagner.

Patriquin wanted to join the army: Author interview with Gary Patriquin, July 22, 2009.

"He was visionary, very cantankerous": Author interview with Marine Maj. John Church, April 25, 2008.

In early December: Bilat report, December 3, 2006.

One day Patriquin strode: E-mail from Maj. Michael Wood, brigade chaplain, September 4, 2009.

17: Justice

Lt. Col. Jim Lechner saw the bomb: The account of the roadside bomb that killed Patriquin, McClung, and Pomante was based on interviews with Lechner and Jensen and Jensen's journal.

Father, you need to go: Author interview with Wood.

That evening Lechner: Author interview with Lechner.

"Why do you Americans": Author interview with Lechner.

I'm going to find: Author interview with Jensen.

It was the first U.S. memorial: Fox News's Oliver North covered the memorial service and allowed the author to view the raw footage.

"We know who did it": Author interview with Lechner.

"You have a smart brain": Author interview with Jensen.

"We hear you got some Americans": Author interview with Lechner.

The initial shock had worn off: Author interview with Jensen.

18: Worthy Allies

Jack Keane, a retired four-star general: Bob Woodward, *The War Within: A Secret White House History 2006–2008* (New York: Simon & Schuster, 2008).

The Ready First had established: Brigade After Action report.

A top-level CIA official: Author interviews with undisclosed officials.

On December 14, Senator John McCain: The account of McCain's visit is based on author interviews with MacFarland, Lee, and Lechner. McCain's office declined to comment.

MacFarland said there were enough: Today, MacFarland says McCain was right about the need for additional troops in Iraq, a strategy that later came to be know as the surge. "I remember thinking that Sen. McCain had already made up his mind about the surge and wasn't really listening to what I had to say about the rest," MacFarland said. "Basically, everything I told him only served to reinforce the idea that we needed more troops. In retrospect, he was more right than I was. I didn't know how thirty thousand [additional troops, which were later sent as part of the surge] could make a decisive change."

They were all supporters: "Military Considers Sending As Many As 35,000 More U.S. Troops to Iraq," *The New York Times*, December 15, 2006.

"Sir, I regret that I did": Senator Joseph Lieberman writing in *The Washington Post*, December 29, 2006.

Capt. Niel Smith took the call: Author interview with Smith.

The American officers dubbed it: Author interview with Lechner.

"I can't tell you exactly what it is": Bob Woodward, *The War Within*.

"Just keep driving on": Author interview with MacFarland.

The brigade had a breakthrough: Author interview with MacFarland.

"As long as they perceived us": Sean MacFarland and Neil Smith, "Anbar Awakens: The Tipping Point," *Military Review*, March-April 2008, 13.

19: The Test

Epigraph: Author interview with Lt. Gen. John Allen, January 12, 2009.

And Petraeus wanted to put Sattar: Author interview with Gen. David Petraeus, Dec. 4, 2009, and author interview with Lechner.

"You've heard of Gen. Petraeus?": Author interview with Lechner.

Petraeus's first trip: The account of Petraeus's visit to Ramadi was based on author interviews with Lechner, Petraeus, and Jensen.

Petraeus had come to Iraq: Author interview with Petraeus.

"A blind man on a dark night": Author interview with Petraeus.

"There was, I think, a sense in '06": Author interview with Allen.

"We've got an issue with this kid": Author interview with Capt. Daniel Enslen, August 7, 2009.

After that he bounced around: "He Should Never Have Gone to Iraq," *Newsweek*, June 30, 2008. Details of Dietrich's background also came from *The Sentinel* in Carlisle, Pennsylvania, and the Harrisburg *Patriot-News*.

"We can all name stories": Quoted in *Patriot-News*.

20: Pure Blood

Epigraph: Poem Lawrence wrote as a dedication to *The Seven Pillars of Wisdom*.

As the marine CH-46 helicopter: The description of President Bush's visit is based on an interview with Lt. Gen. John Allen and a pool report from Michael A. Fletcher of *The Washington Post*. The pool report was provided by the George W. Bush Presidential Library.

As the sheiks waited anxiously: The account of the meeting with Bush and Iraqi officials was provided by Allen, who was in the room.

Johnson tried to change the subject: Author interview with Lt. Col. Miciotto Johnson, April 21, 2009.

Sattar was still pumped up: Author interview with Matt Sanchez, September 7, 2009.

"They could have caused": Intelligence report dated July 5, 2007.

The lopsided U.S. victory: Author interview with Johnson and a written summary of the Donkey Island battle by Task Force 1–77.

In July 2007 a suicide: Declassified Second Marine Expeditionary Force report, dated July 7, 2007.

Al-Qaeda wanted to: Declassified intelligence report dated July 16–17, 2007.

"The loss of the Euphrates": Author interview with Gen. David Petraeus, September 13, 2007.

"Once you attain power": Author interview with William McCallister, February 2, 2009.

Sattar had climbed into his unarmored: The account of Sattar's death comes from a number of sources, including interviews with Johnson, Allen, and others, as well as declassified intelligence reports.

They had packed sixty to eighty pounds of homemade explosive: Declassified intelligence report.

The day after his testimony: Author interview with Col. Steve Boylan, May 12, 2009.

In Baghdad, the insurgents: Declassified message dated September 13, 2007.

"Although they killed Sattar": Alissa J. Rubin, "Sunni Sheik Who Backed U.S. in Iraq Is Killed," *The New York Times*, September 14, 2007.

After his brigade left Iraq: MacFarland's return trip to Ramadi was recounted by him.

SELECTED BIBLIOGRAPHY

Asprey, Robert B. *War in the Shadows: The Guerrilla in History.* Vols. I and II. Garden City, New York: Doubleday & Company, 1975.

Batatu, Hanna. *The Old Social Classes and the Revolutionary Movements of Iraq: A Study of Iraq's Old Landed and Commercial Classes and of Its Communists, Ba'thists, and Free Officers.* London: Saqi Books, 2004.

Couch, Dick. *The Sheriff of Ramadi: Navy SEALs and the Winning of al-Anbar.* Annapolis, Maryland: Naval Institute Press, 2008.

Haldane, Sir Aylmer L. *The Insurrection in Mesopotamia 1920,* London: Imperial War Museum, Department of Printed Books, 2005.

Howell, Georgina. *Gertrude Bell: Queen of the Desert, Shaper of Nations.* New York: Farrar, Straus and Giroux, 2006.

Jabar, Faleh A., and Hosham Dawod, eds. *Tribes and Power: Nationalism and Ethnicity in the Middle East.* London: Saqi Books, 2003.

Marr, Phebe. *The Modern History of Iraq.* Boulder, Colorado: Westview Press, 2004.

Ricks, Thomas E. *The Gamble: General David Petraeus and the American Military Adventure in Iraq, 2006–2008.* New York: Penguin Press, 2009.

Robinson, Linda. *Tell Me How This Ends: General David Petraeus and the Search for a Way Out of Iraq.* New York: PublicAffairs, 2008.

Sluglett, Peter. *Britain in Iraq: Contriving King and Country.* New York: Columbia University Press, 2007.

West, Bing. *No True Glory: A Frontline Account of the Battle for Fallujah.* New York: Bantam, 2005.

West, Bing. *The Strongest Tribe: War, Politics, and the Endgame in Iraq.* New York: Random House, 2008.

Woodward, Bob. *The War Within: A Secret White House History 2006–2008.* New York: Simon & Schuster, 2008.

WHERE THEY ARE NOW

Al-Rishawi, Ahmad. Replaced his brother as head of the Awakening movement after Sattar was assassinated; he has emerged as a major political figure in Iraq and is aligned with Prime Minister Nouri al-Maliki.

Allen, John. Promoted to lieutenant general and was handpicked by Gen. David Petraeus to serve as his deputy at Central Command in Tampa, Florida.

Al-Alwani, Mamoun Sami Rashid. Mamoun formed an alliance with Awakening tribal leaders. He is no longer governor, but has a seat on the provincial council.

Bajema, Mike. Promoted to major, he is attending the Maritime Advanced Warfighting School at Newport, Rhode Island.

Cadena, Jesus. Promoted to staff sergeant, Cadena remains in the army on active duty.

Conway, James. Promoted to a four-star general; now commandant of the U.S. Marine Corps.

Davis, Tom. Spent fifteen months at Walter Reed Army Hospital; left leg amputated. Initially stayed in the army and taught at Fort Benning, Georgia; now retired on 100 percent disability and lives in Indiana.

Deane, Tony. Promoted to colonel and assigned to command a training team at the Combined Arms Center at Fort Leavenworth, Kansas;

travels the country, teaching counterinsurgency operations to brigades about to deploy to Iraq or Afghanistan.

Dickerson, Jason. Left the active duty army and is attending the University of Texas at Dallas; is considering a career as a physician or physician's assistant.

Ferry, Chuck. Was offered command of a brigade, but turned down the promotion and retired from the army to spend more time with his family.

Gronski, John. Promoted to brigadier general in the National Guard; in civilian life is a business consultant.

Jensen, Sterling. Returned to Iraq in August 2008 as a foreign area officer advising the marine command at Camp Fallujah. Back in the United States he received a master's degree from Johns Hopkins School of Advanced International Studies.

Lechner, Jim. Assigned to Special Operations Command, he served a tour in Afghanistan where he helped work on an initiative to organize and support the tribes.

MacFarland, Sean. Promoted to brigadier general by a selection board led by Gen. David Petraeus; assigned as commander of Joint Task Force North at Fort Bliss, Texas.

Mattis, James. Promoted to a four-star general; commander of Joint Forces Command in Norfolk, Virginia.

Reist, David. Retired from the Marine Corps and now works as an analyst for the Potomac Institute for Policy Studies.

Tedesco, V. J. Promoted to colonel, he is serving as the chief of plans at U.S. Army Forces Command in Atlanta. Among other things, he is responsible for identifying and ordering the deployment of all army units headed to the wars in Iraq and Afghanistan.

Zilmer, Richard. Promoted to lieutenant general, he is now deputy commandant for manpower and reserve affairs at Headquarters, Marine Corps.

ACKNOWLEDGMENTS

This book would not have been possible without the help and cooperation of dozens of soldiers and marines of the Ready First Brigade and their parent headquarters, the First Marine Expeditionary Force. These soldiers and marines gave generously of their time and asked nothing in return, other than that I try to tell their story honestly. I hope I have done them and their remarkable story justice.

It would be impossible to single everyone of them out here, but a few merit mention. The brigade commander, Sean MacFarland, not only gave generously of his time, but also supported my efforts by encouraging subordinates to tell their stories. Tony Deane spent hours with me on the telephone and in person, walking me through the events of 2006. MacFarland's deputy, Jim Lechner, took time to meet with me wherever he was, including on a recent tour in Afghanistan. Sterling Jensen, who served as Lechner's translator, probably understands the Awakening as well as any American. Sterling's Arabic skills and deep understanding of Iraqi culture and people allowed him to see the tribal revolt from the Iraqi perspective. He generously shared his insights with me. The Iraqi perspective of the war is another book. I hope Sterling writes it.

There were so many acts—big and small—of heroism in Ramadi and other parts of Iraq. I captured but a few. Men like Tom Davis, Jason Dickerson, and Jesus Cadena shared their stories. Their acts were inspiring and I thank them for agreeing to talk about them.

I owe much to the families of the fallen. Tracy Tribble, whose son Brett was killed shortly after the brigade arrived in Ramadi, talked to me about her son, who had found a home and a calling in the army. Gary Patriquin helped me understand his son Travis, an Arabic speaker who formed a warm bond with the sheiks and proved one of the most remarkable figures in this story. America owes much to these and other families.

Marine Lt. Gen. John Allen spent hours with me on the phone and then agreed to review relevant passages of the book for accuracy. His public affairs officer, Marine Lt. Col. Joseph Kloppel, was a big help as well.

Gen. David Petraeus spent time with me on the telephone and took me along on several trips when he was commanding forces in Iraq. Col. Steve Boylan, Gen. Petraeus's public affairs officer in Iraq, never turned down a request and worked tirelessly to tell the army's story.

Zaid Sabah, who worked for *USA Today* and later *The Washington Post* in Iraq, was my teacher, mentor, and guide through countless visits to Iraq. He also helped me with this book. Over the course of six years and numerous trips to Iraq I came to love the country and its people. Their resilence, sense of humor, and sheer fortitude in the face of enormous challanges are humbling. Zaid embodies all of that.

Carol Stevens and Owen Ullmann, both of *USA Today*, generously allowed me time off to pursue this book.

Col. Gary Montgomery and Chief Warrant Officer 4 Timothy Mc-Williams of the Marine Corps History Division have done remarkable work interviewing Iraqi and Marine Corps leaders in Anbar. I could not have done this book without use of their research. They were both also generous in sharing their insights with me.

This book touches on only a small fraction of what went on in Iraq during a long war. Even many people who played significant roles in Anbar do not appear in the book. As a deputy commander for First

Marine Expeditionary Force in 2006, Maj. Gen. Robert Neller played a prominent role in bolstering Iraqi police and other security forces and guided countless operations there. In 1981 he was a young company commander when a very green second lieutenant reported for duty at Company A, First Battalion, First Marines. I was one of hundreds of young marines who were touched by Maj. Gen. Neller's leadership over the course of his brilliant career. Our lives are better for it.

I cannot imagine a better place from which to write a book than the Woodrow Wilson International Center for Scholars. I owe Lucy Jilka, Mike Van Dusen, and Lee Hamilton a debt of gratitude for hosting me at the center and providing an environment that was both supportive and inspiring. My assistant there, Matt Irvine, was a tireless researcher, a smart analyst, and a teriffic colleague. This book owes much to Matt's insights and ability to track down information, no matter how difficult.

My agent, Scott Miller of Trident Media, saw value in my idea and provided critical help in shaping it. Editor Marc Resnick has the values every writer wants in an editor: patience, understanding, and flawless judgment.

Nancy came up with the perfect name for this book. She also provided invaluable editing and advice, influencing this book in immeasurable ways.

Finally, Michelle and Sally: Thank you for everything.

IN MEMORIAM

James W. Michaels

1921–2007

American Field Service

India-Burma Theater, World War II

Robert A. Matthews

1921–1944

Second Lieutenant, Army Air Corps